STRATEGIES TO MAKE YOU SMARTER THAN THE BANKS, MORTGAGE COMPANIES, AND THE TAX MAN, TOO

With mortgage interest rates at near-record lows, more and more people find the pinnacle of the American Dream—home ownership—within their reach. But how do you go about getting the best possible mortgage? What costs besides interest rates do you need to be aware of? Should you refinance an existing mortgage? How can you handle problems with your credit so they won't keep you from getting a loan?

Written in clear, accessible language, *The Mortgage Handbook* guides consumers through the maze of home financing issues, and will help them make good, money-saving choices. Personal finance expert William Kent Brunette has written a practical book filled with work sheets and checklists that put power in the hands of the consumers when they're bargaining for a mortgage.

Since buying a home is probably the most significant financial commitment people ever make, this absolutely essential resource for both current homeowners and first-time buyers will help to insure that they'll get the best possible deal for themselves and their families.

W9-AWS-748

THE MORTGAGE HANDBOOK

Protecting Yourself and Getting the Most for Your Home Financing Dollar

WILLIAM KENT BRUNETTE is a lawyer and consultant who writes frequently about personal finance. He served for fourteen years as the chief consumer lobbyist for the 34 million–member American Association of Retired Persons (AARP), is the author of *Conquer Your Debt*, co-author of *Money in the Bank*, and a contributing editior to *Court TV's Cradle-to-Grave Legal Survival Guide.* He lives in Washington, D.C.

THE MORTGAGE HANDBOOK

Protecting Yourself and Getting the
Most for Your Home Financing Dollar

William Kent Brunette

A PLUME BOOK

PLUME
Published by the Penguin Group
Penguin Books USA Inc., 375 Hudson Street,
New York, New York 10014, U.S.A.
Penguin Books Ltd, 27 Wrights Lane,
London W8 5TZ, England
Penguin Books Australia Ltd, Ringwood,
Victoria, Australia
Penguin Books Canada Ltd, 10 Alcorn Avenue,
Toronto, Ontario, Canada M4V 3B2
Penguin Books (N.Z.) Ltd, 182–190 Wairau Road,
Auckland 10, New Zealand

Penguin Books Ltd, Registered Offices:
Harmondsworth, Middlesex, England

First published by Plume, an imprint of Dutton Signet,
a division of Penguin Books USA Inc.

First Printing, April, 1997
10 9 8 7 6 5 4 3 2 1

Ⓟ   REGISTERED TRADEMARK—MARCA REGISTRADA

LIBRARY OF CONGRESS CATALOGING-IN-PUBLICATION DATA:

Brunette, William Kent.
    The mortgage hanbook : protecting yourself and getting the most for your home financing dollar / William Kent Brunette.
        p.   cm.
    ISBN 0-452-27710-8
    1. Mortgages—United States.   I. Title.
HG4655.B78   1997
332.7'22—dc20   96-41436
                                                                CIP

Printed in the United States of America
Set in New Baskerville
Designed by Leonard Telesca

DEDICATION

My mom, Lois Evelyn (Bush) Brunette, lost her battle with cancer while this book was being written. But the lessons she and my dad, William Jacob Brunette, tried to teach me—to plan ahead, do your homework, and shop around—live on.

ACKNOWLEDGMENTS

This book would not have been possible without the significant contributions of Roberto Kramer and Mawtha Beaches. Thanks also go to Margot Saunders, Zina Greene, and Dave Affeldt whose knowledge and expertise are reflected on many of these pages. In addition, Deb Brody, my editor, and her assistant, Jennifer Moore, are to be commended for their dedication to this project. As always, I am grateful to Stuart Krichevsky, my literary agent, for all of his efforts on my behalf. Special thanks also go to my family and friends whose love, support, understanding, and encouragement helped to make this book a reality.

Contents

10. Applying for a Mortgage   102

11. After You Submit Your Application   112

12. Closing Costs   122

Introduction

Mortgage rates have been fairly low in recent years and may be low for quite some time. In this environment, opportunities abound for you to:

- Refinance your existing higher-rate mortgage
- Afford a first home
- Move up or down in the mortgage market

Low interest rates are placing home ownership within the reach of more and more Americans. Indeed, you may have thought you would never be able to afford a home, but now you're seriously considering buying one. Or, maybe you missed out on the refinancing boom several years ago, and have not yet refinanced your existing high-rate mortgage. You may still be able to benefit from lower interest rates. Homeowners who do this can rack up substantial cost savings, reduce monthly payments, and lower considerably a home's ultimate purchase price. For example, refinancing a $100,000 mortgage at 7.5 percent instead of 9.5 percent can reduce the monthly payment by $170 and save the homeowner several thousand dollars in the process.

While there are some great deals to be had in the mortgage marketplace, you may find yourself wandering around in a mortgage maze. Even if you've been through the home-financing process before, you may find yourself at a loss. That's because mortgage products have changed considerably in recent years. There is a tremendous variety of complex and confusing mortgage products on the market today. Not only are there many different types of mortgages (fixed rate, adjustable rate, balloon payment, graduated payment, wrap-around mortgages, reverse mortgages, etc.), but there is tremendous variation within each category. Whether it's a one-year adjustable rate, a fifteen- or thirty-year fixed rate, a combi-nation seven/twenty-three, or another type of mortgage, you need to understand the differences and to be able to pick a home-financing product specifically tailored to your needs and financial circumstances.

While the interest rate is perhaps the most important mort-gage pricing component, other costs are important as well. These include: points, closing costs, fees for application, title, attorneys, lender's agent, and others. These costs, which vary greatly, further add to confusion and increase financial out-lays. In addition to cost issues, you may be subjected to varying terms, conditions, and practices that can adversely affect you. For example, your closing date may be pushed back beyond the "lock-in" date. This may strap you with a higher interest rate and other costs once you finally make it to settlement. Already difficult circumstances are exacerbated by problems with mortgage brokers. Even after the deal has been com-pleted and the paperwork has been signed, there is nothing to prevent your lender from selling your mortgage to another lender in the secondary market. Thus, even though your mort-gage contract is with one company, you may suddenly find yourself making payments to someone else, possibly a lender in a distant state.

A mortgage is probably the single most expensive product you will ever purchase. By paying greater attention to home-financing costs, you can save thousands, if not tens of thou-sands, of dollars. You can easily shave considerable costs off your mortgage simply by learning more about products around you, shopping around for the best deals, finding the shortest-term mortgages you can afford, and purchasing the lowest-rate mortgages available.

Since a mortgage represents an ongoing financial obligation, it has a significant impact upon a homeowner's life for years to come. Indeed, mortgage expenses, which take a considerable bite out of a monthly budget, often dictate how much money is available for other activities. As a result, you assume huge risks when making home-financing choices. Good mortgage decisions can serve you well and save you lots of money. Bad mortgage decisions can haunt you for years to come and wind up costing you a bundle. In today's highly competitive mortgage market, the dream of home ownership does not have to come with a dear price tag attached. You should be able to get a very favorable mortgage that allows you not only to buy a house but also gives you the flexibility to accomplish your dreams and to enjoy other aspects of your life at the same time.

With so much resting in the balance, you need a road map to assist you along the mortgage route. *The Mortgage Handbook* provides timely, valuable, comprehensive, and pragmatic information to assist you in sorting through the confusion of today's home-financing market. It does this in an interesting, enjoyable, easy-to-understand, and user-friendly fashion. It brings the complex and intimidating world of mortgages into crystal-clear focus. It helps you understand myriad home-financing issues confronting you and allows you to benefit from current offerings.

The Mortgage Handbook takes you by the hand and leads you through the mortgage maze. It shows you the steps you need to take at every turn to protect yourself and to maximize your position. It helps you anticipate lender concerns and avoid needless hassles. It also shows you how to avoid common pitfalls and where to complain if you encounter problems. It apprises you of your rights and how to enforce them. The book empowers you with the resources you need to chart your own course. It is chock full of good ideas for anyone who currently has or may be contemplating a mortgage.

The Mortgage Handbook gives current and potential home-

owners a fighting chance to emerge triumphant from the mortgage revolution of the nineties. By providing you with fingertip
access to sound information on all of the home-financing issues
you will likely encounter, the book places ordinary citizens in
much stronger bargaining positions when dealing with mortgage lenders.

CHAPTER 1

Beware of Obstacles

Audrey and Randall are confused by all of the mortgage offerings they've encountered. Their realtor has referred them to a friend of his, a nice young mortgage lender who seems to know what he's talking about. As they see it, there's really no need for them to develop an independent knowledge of the mortgage market since they have a seemingly reliable source at their disposal.

People are intimidated by financial purchase decisions. Often complex and confusing, some prefer to avoid financial decisions like the plague. The mother of all financial decisions is the home mortgage. Indeed, a mortgage represents the single largest purchase most people will make in their lifetimes. While vast numbers of people are scared to death of shopping for a credit card or changing bank accounts, many become apoplectic when faced with financial decisions associated with buying a home.

Most people don't want to belabor the mortgage decision. Instead of approaching it rationally and carefully thinking through every decision, many people simply want to get the mortgage process over with as quickly as possible. They want to rush through it so they don't have to deal with it anymore.

The problem is that most people develop only a rudimentary knowledge of the basics of mortgage finance, so they feel comfortable making decisions. For example, a friend recently told me that her comfort level when buying her first home soared once she finally understood the concept of *points* after it had been explained to her by a real estate agent. Since mortgage issues have such a long-term impact on your life, you cannot base these all-important decisions on a limited knowledge of the mortgage-granting process. You simply cannot allow yourself to be content with a superficial search for mortgage information. Instead of surveying a limited range of options, you need to actively consider every alternative available to you. Indeed, the best mortgage may be the one you learn about tomorrow or the next day as you become more knowledgeable about the differences in the plethora of products currently available.

A highly successful businessman friend of mine recently told me about how he had become a successful investor. I was amazed at how much time and attention he pays to investment issues. He religiously reads newspapers to glean information; he subscribes to stock market-monitoring services; he watches and listens to financial television and radio shows to assess what others are advising. After doing all of this, *he then talks with his stockbroker.* Even though my friend is not in the investment business, he takes the time and trouble to learn more about investment issues that are important to him. He also doesn't take his stockbroker's advice at face value. He does his homework and has enough knowledge to evaluate recommendations made independently.

The same standard should apply to anyone considering a home mortgage. Rest assured, you do not have to become a financial guru, appear on the morning or evening news programs, or have a syndicated column that explains complex financial issues to the masses. You just need to learn more about these decisions that will heavily impact your life for years to come.

Yes, it may be far more stressful to learn more about mortgage products than to avoid them. The multitude of available choices will probably further heighten your anxiety levels. You will, no doubt, be confronted with a series of costly alternatives that are difficult to compare. But the risks of not doing anything or accepting something simply because it appears to satisfy an immediate need can be quite costly.

If you are contemplating buying a home and selecting a mortgage, consider the following recommendations:

Don't be lazy.   The chances are probably pretty good that if you don't take the time and trouble to delve into mortgage issues and determine what's best for you, no one else will. It's not like the phone is going to ring and some soothsayer will pronounce, "Take the ARM with XYZ Mortgage." These decisions don't just fall from the sky. Mortgage issues are not to be taken lightly or dealt with casually. Procrastination should be avoided. You need to affirmatively deal with mortgage-related issues.

Don't shift responsibility.   You are responsible for all of your mortgage-related decisions. You're flirting with disaster if you entrust mortgage decisions to someone who you feel is highly knowledgeable about mortgage issues. You cannot make decisions solely on the advice of mortgage bankers, mortgage brokers, builders, home sellers, or real estate agents. All of these people have a vested interest in and will benefit from your acceptance of their sales pitch. Granted, many of these people may be very knowledgeable about mortgage-related issues. But you simply cannot take their advice at face value. You need to delve into mortgage issues so you gain more than just a cursory understanding of these important topics. You need to develop an independent knowledge of mortgage issues that builds on and complements the information provided by others. You need to be in a position where you can evaluate information provided by others.

Don't take the easy way out.   Many people make the common mistake of opting for the most readily available alternative. Don't allow yourself to become complacent or content with a mortgage product that is simply "good enough." Go out and find the "best" product available, one that is precisely suited to your unique needs. The failure to do so could cost you tens of thousands of dollars over the life of the mortgage. This is money that could probably be devoted to many other worthwhile causes and needs in your life.

Take your time. You don't want to rush into a mortgage decision. To avoid this, give yourself ample time to survey all of the possibilities. If you need further information, make a deliberate attempt to find the missing piece of the puzzle. Putting yourself in a state of panic may effectively paralyze you from shopping around for the best deal. In such circumstances, you might accept what's available, not necessarily what's advisable.

Do your homework. Learn more about the different types of mortgage products currently available. While this book provides a wealth of information, you might also consider consulting a variety of other sources. The financial sections of many newspapers, personal-finance magazines, television and radio shows and reports often highlight mortgage-interest rates. Many newspapers routinely feature periodic listings of mortgage-interest rates available from local lenders. You might also contact or pick up information from local mortgage providers in your area to learn more about locally available products. Bear in mind, however, that if you provide your name, address, and telephone number, you'll probably be contacted by sales representatives who are anxious to get your business.

You may also live in a community where a "home buying fair" may be sponsored. For example, the Federal National Home Mortgage Corporation (also known as Fannie Mae) occasionally sponsors such fairs around the country. At these fairs, different mortgage providers set up booths, provide free literature, application forms, and other information. Computer equipment is often available to pre-qualify prospective home buyers. Since these fairs represent tremendous one-stop shopping opportunities, be on the lookout for one in your local area and make plans to attend.

Shop around. There are many different mortgage-financing options for you to consider. How will you ever be able to deter-

mine what's best for you if you don't go out and shop around?
You don't want to offer yourself up as the "sacrificial offering"
to some mortgage lender who'll be able to send his daughter
through college on the money he'll make off your loan.
Instead, you need to search out ways to maximize your position
and look out for your own best interest.

CHAPTER 2

Preparing Yourself for Home Ownership

Lois and Bill have decided that they want to buy their first house in five years. In the meantime they've developed a plan to save $20,000 to cover the down payment they'll need to buy their home.

Cyndie went on a spending spree with her credit cards for a couple of years after she got out of college. While most of her friends are now buying houses, Cyndie is strapped with so much debt that she cannot find a mortgage lender who'll make her a loan on a house.

Don and Cathy are newlyweds who are so much in love they can't see straight. They want to buy a house to live in and get out of Don's cramped apartment, which is overrun with stuff. But they don't have a clue about how much money they'll need to make a down payment on a home.

You need to develop a series of goals to prepare yourself for home ownership. First, you need to know how much money will be expected in up-front costs. This can be a major obstacle for many people because of the dollar figure involved. For most people it requires a conscientious effort to save money. It may entail putting yourself on a budget and forgoing desired but not required expenditures. You also need to look at your financial picture. Are you overextended or do you owe too much money? How does your credit report look? What can you do to enhance your chances of getting a mortgage loan approved?

Obvious questions arise. How do you get to where you need to be? How do you get out of debt and start saving? How do you go about socking away enough money for the down payment? How do you accomplish all of these things while still allowing yourself to enjoy your life?

All of these things can be accomplished if you put your mind to it. The steps outlined in this chapter will help to make you as financially attractive as possible and will enable you to put your best foot forward when trying to convince mortgage lenders that you're a viable candidate for a loan.

Step 1. Conduct a Personal Assessment of Your Current Circumstances

At the outset you need to obtain an accurate assessment of your financial circumstances. Take an inventory of your assets and liabilities. Create a financial balance sheet that shows exactly where you stand. Identify areas where improvements can be made.

Where Is Your Money Going?

While you may have a vague notion of where your hard-earned money is going, you probably need to understand precisely where it is being spent. The table below should help you figure out what percentages of your take-home pay are allocated to various types of expenditures. Fill in the actual amount you spend each month for each category. Then divide this amount by your total monthly take-home pay. Multiply the answer by 100. This will give you the percentage of income you spend on each item per month. After doing these calculations, compare your expenditures with recommended spending levels.

Example: If your monthly mortgage payment is $400, and

your monthly take-home pay is $1,200, your actual housing percentage is: $400 ÷ $1,200 = .33 × 100 = 33%

Recommended Guidelines for Spending

Category of Expenditure	Actual Amounts	Actual Percentages	Recommended Percentages
Housing (including rent or mortgage payments, condo/coop fees, utilities, supplies)	$ _____	_____ %	33–35%
Food	_____	_____	20–26
Transportation (including gas/oil, public transportation)	_____	_____	7–9
Clothing (including dry cleaning/laundry)	_____	_____	6–12
Medical (including dental, eyewear, prescriptions, health insurance, out-of-pocket costs)	_____	_____	6–8
Auto insurance	_____	_____	2–3
Life insurance	_____	_____	2–5
Education/Advancement	_____	_____	2–3
Credit obligations (including credit card and car payments)	_____	_____	15–18
Savings	_____	_____	2–10
Recreation/ Entertainment/ Child care	_____	_____	4–6
Church charities	_____	_____	4–10

With the exception of the savings category, higher-than-recommended percentages may indicate excessive spending and an area in which expenditures should be reevaluated or controlled. If your percentages are lower than or equal to those recommended, you fall within the recommended spending guidelines for that category.

These figures should be viewed only as guidelines. Individual circumstances will obviously vary. For example, if you have three young children at home, the percentage you pay on child care and related expenses is probably considerably higher than those recommended. Similarly, if you live in an area where housing costs are extremely high, your housing costs may necessarily consume a disproportionate share of your take-home pay.

How Much Do You Owe?

To determine the extent of your current indebtedness, list all creditors to whom you owe money. After each debt has been listed, add all outstanding current balances to determine your total indebtedness.

Your Indebtedness

Name of Creditor/Type of Loan	Outstanding Balance
_____	$ _____
_____	_____
_____	_____
_____	_____
_____	_____
_____	_____
_____	_____
Total Indebtedness =	$ _____

How Much Have You Saved?

Short-term savings is the amount of money you could easily get your hands on should you need it in an emergency. This is money that is available to help you respond to things like family illness or home and car repairs. This would include money in checking and savings accounts, short-term certificates of deposit, mutual funds, stocks and bonds, and other resources that are readily available to you. To help you gauge where you stand regarding short-term savings, list all of your current savings and investment-account balances on the chart below. After you've entered these figures, total your available short-term savings.

Short-term Savings

Place Deposited/Type of Investment	Account Balance/ Value of Investment
_____	$ _____
_____	_____
_____	_____
_____	_____
_____	_____
_____	_____
_____	_____

Total Short-term Savings = $ _____

Mid-term savings might be held in savings accounts, longer-term certificates of deposits, and other such obligations. Mid-term savings is any money you have socked away for special life events (e.g., educational expenses for children, down payment on a home, money set aside to care for your parents). Record your mid-term savings balances in the spaces provided below and then total them.

Mid-term Savings

Place Deposited/Type of Investment/Purpose	Account Balance/ Value of Investment
_____	$ _____
_____	_____
_____	_____
_____	_____
_____	_____

Total Mid-term Savings = $ _____

Long-term savings represents another important area of financial planning. This is money you have stashed away as your retirement nest egg. This includes balances in individual retirement accounts, simplified employer pension plans, Keogh accounts, 401(k) plans, voluntary and regular pension plans, and other retirement accounts. Because these long-term savings should be maintained for your retirement and should not be used for a home purchase, they should not be included in your calculations of available resources.

Step 2. Learn the Basics of Personal Finance

Few consumers have a working knowledge of essential, important consumer financial information. For example, many Americans could not tell you how much debt is too much, identify the recommended savings cushion for meeting short-term needs, or come up with a ball park figure about how much money is needed for a down-payment on a house. This is important information few people, regrettably, have ever contemplated.

How Much Should You Owe?

Your debt-to-income ratio should not be out of balance or exceed tolerable limits. Installment debts (like automobile loans, credit cards, store charge accounts, personal loans, or student loans) should not exceed more than 20 percent of your annual take-home pay. Anything in excess of this is generally considered an overextension of credit obligations. While 20 percent represents the tolerable maximum, a 15 percent limit is recommended as a more comfortable level of indebtedness. At 15 percent, your debts will be more manageable than at a higher rate, and you will have greater flexibility in meeting any unplanned or sudden expenditures. With debts at this level or lower of your annual take-home pay, you'll be better able to make your mortgage payments and should have fewer demands placed on your available resources.

The chart below indicates tolerable limits on credit obligations for different income levels. You should determine your income level and identify your "comfortable" and "maximum" credit-obligation amounts. These should then be compared with the actual amount of your total indebtedness.

Suggested Income-to-Debt Ratios by Income Level

Take-Home Pay Per Month	Per Year	Comfortable 15%	Maximum 20%
$250	$3,000	$450	$600
500	6,000	900	1,200
750	9,000	1,350	1,800
1,000	12,000	1,800	2,400
1,250	15,000	2,250	3,000
1,500	18,000	2,700	3,600
1,750	21,000	3,150	4,200
2,000	24,000	3,600	4,800
2,250	27,000	4,050	5,400
2,500	30,000	4,500	6,000
2,750	33,000	4,950	6,600
3,000	36,000	5,400	7,200
3,250	39,000	5,850	7,800
3,500	42,000	6,300	8,400
3,750	45,000	6,750	9,000
4,000	48,000	7,200	9,600
4,250	51,000	7,650	10,200
4,500	54,000	8,100	10,800
4,750	57,000	8,550	11,400

Once your percentages have been determined, they should be evaluated as follows:

- If you exceed the 20 percent level, you should make every effort to bring your total indebtedness down to or below the maximum tolerable amount for your income category.

- If you are between the 15 and 20 percent levels, you should not assume any new credit obligations and strive toward the lower goal.

- If you fall below 15 percent, you probably are not over-extended. However, you should become familiar with the tolerable limits on credit obligations for your income category and be wary of any obligation that would force you to become overextended.

The 15 and 20 percent limits are flexible and are intended only as guidelines for assessing general credit conditions. Your specific situation should be taken into consideration when applying the guidelines. For example, because purchasing a new car may make you exceed the above guidelines, you may need to be cautious with future purchases, making certain to keep your obligations within your ability to repay.

How Much Should You Save?

It is recommended that you have a *short-term savings* cushion of from three to six months of your annual take-home pay available to assist you in responding to life's exigencies. Use the savings figure you calculated above to determine the percentage of your annual take-home pay you currently have available in short-term savings. To assist you, the table below identifies recommended savings levels for different income levels.

Suggested Short-term Savings-to-Pay Ratios by Income Level

| Take-Home Pay | | Minimum Recommended | |
Per Month	Per Year	3 Months	6 Months
$250	$3,000	$750	$1,500
500	6,000	1,500	3,000

Take-Home Pay		Minimum Recommended	
Per Month	Per Year	3 Months	6 Months
750	9,000	2,250	4,500
1,000	12,000	3,000	6,000
1,250	15,000	3,750	7,500
1,500	18,000	4,500	9,000
1,750	21,000	5,250	10,500
2,000	24,000	6,000	12,000
2,250	27,000	6,750	13,500
2,500	30,000	7,500	15,000
2,750	33,000	8,250	16,500
3,000	36,000	9,000	18,000
3,250	39,000	9,750	19,500
3,500	42,000	10,500	21,000
3,750	45,000	11,250	22,500

Size of Required Down Payment

One of your most important *mid-term goals* is to amass funds for a down payment on a home. That's because a down payment of anywhere from 10 to 20 percent of the purchase price of the home is normally required at the time of purchase. In addition, closing costs usually run about 4 percent of the home's purchase price. Depending upon the pricing of the mortgage you ultimately receive, you may also need to pay points and other costs up-front as part of your initial outlays. Given this, your initial costs may be greater than indicated below. The following chart gives you a pretty good idea of the up-front costs normally required.

Home Purchase Expenses

Purchase Price of Home	10% Down Payment	20% Down Payment	4% Closing Costs	Total Up-front Costs
$50,000	$5,000	$10,000	$2,000	$7,000–12,000
60,000	6,000	12,000	2,400	8,400–14,400
70,000	7,000	14,000	2,800	9,800–16,800

Purchase Price of Home	10% Down Payment	20% Down Payment	4% Closing Costs	Total Up-front Costs
80,000	8,000	16,000	3,200	11,200–19,200
90,000	9,000	18,000	3,600	12,600–21,600
100,000	10,000	20,000	4,000	14,000–24,000
110,000	11,000	22,000	4,400	15,400–26,400
120,000	12,000	24,000	4,800	16,800–28,800
130,000	13,000	26,000	5,200	18,200–31,200
140,000	14,000	28,000	5,600	19,500–33,600
150,000	15,000	30,000	6,000	21,000–36,000

As the above chart demonstrates, the dream of home ownership comes with a hefty price tag attached. Depending upon your circumstances, you'll need to cough up a sizable amount. For example, if you need $12,500 in up-front purchase costs, you'd have to put away $2,200 a year (assuming an average annual return of 7 percent) for five years, or you'd need $6,000 saved over each of two years. Similarly, if your goal is to come up with $30,000 in up-front purchase costs, you'll need to sock away $2,200 a year over ten years, or to save $5,200 a year over a five-year period to purchase your new home.

Step 3. Identify Financial Goals

Once your positions have been determined above, you next need to identify financial goals. For example, if you lack an adequate savings cushion, steps should be identified to begin the saving process immediately (assuming there are no debt problems to be corrected first). An initial modest savings program might be developed to demonstrate that savings can easily be accomplished and that earnings can quickly mount up. After a period of time at the initial savings level, adjustments might be made to accomplish even greater savings on a regular basis.

Step 4. Develop a Realistic Plan for Accomplishing Your Goals

The first thing you will probably need to do in developing a plan for accomplishing your goals is to create a budget. This will entail reevaluating your spending patterns and identifying ways of maximizing your available resources. This budget, which is based on household values and priorities, should allow for the accomplishment of financial and personal goals. It must take into consideration the needs and views of every member of your household.

Your budget should not be developed hastily; take whatever time you need to think each decision through. Keep it simple. Your budget must be practical; do not strap yourself down to a plan you cannot realistically achieve. Since you cannot possibly anticipate all your upcoming spending needs, your budget must be flexible—you must allow room for give and take. Chances are good that if you devise a three-year budget today, it will need to be adjusted to reflect changed circumstances at least several times during its existence.

You should try to reduce expenditures in every budgetary category. Many expenditures will probably have to be curtailed—by cutting back on or doing without things you have become accustomed to. However, there may be little flexibility with some expenses, like rent, existing mortgage, or car payments. Therefore, the areas where spending reductions can be made will probably be dictated by the structure of your current expenses. After expenses have been reduced and minimal spending levels identified for each budget category, the remainder of your available funds should be earmarked for your financial goals.

Put your budget in writing and share it with the members of your household. It is important for everyone affected to be familiar with budgetary expectations. If different members will be responsible for different expenses, identify who will be handling which budget items.

Remember, you and the members of your household are responsible for the success or failure of your budget. If you are tempted to make an unbudgeted expenditure, think about the impact such an expenditure will have on your plan. Impulse buying or unnecessary purchases must be avoided. Purchases should be made only after careful thought, planning, and consideration of their repercussions.

Use the following form to create your own household budget.

Your Household Budget

Gross Income

Salary/Wages	$ _____
Investment income	_____
Social Security/Disability	_____
Pensions and annuities	_____
Alimony/Child support	_____
Unemployment	_____
Other	_____
Total Gross Income	_____

Deductions from Gross Income

Taxes	_____
Insurance	_____
Savings	_____
Other	_____
Total Deductions	_____

Available (Net) Income

Subtract applicable deductions from gross income	_____

Expenses

Housing (rent, mortgage, maintenance)	_____
Utilities	_____

Expenses

Household   _____
Food   _____
Transportation   _____
Taxes (like property taxes)   _____
Insurance   _____
Children   _____
Clothing   _____
Medical   _____
Education   _____
Savings   _____
Charitable   _____
Personal   _____
Other   _____
Total Expenses   _____

Money Available for Financial Goals

Subtract expenses from available income $ _____

After you've created a budget, you next need to develop a plan for accomplishing your financial goals within your budgetary constraints. If you have a significant amount of outstanding debt, your first priority should be to bring your indebtedness within tolerable limits.

Step 5. Shop Around for the Best Financial Products

Credit, savings, and investment products of varying shapes and sizes abound. Familiar products may be changing; new products are emerging daily. In this environment you need to: do your homework, learn more about different offerings, shop around, and find products that are best suited to your unique circumstances, spending patterns, savings and investment objectives, and lifestyle.

Step 6. Earmark Savings for Different Purposes

After you've developed financial goals and devised a plan for achieving them, you need to earmark your savings for different purposes. There are some very practical and compelling reasons for doing this. It's probably not a good idea to throw all of your savings into a common account. You're likely to forget which money goes to which purpose. If you've commingled your "mad money" with money that has been designated for a down payment on a home, you may be tempted to use this money for a variety of unintended purposes. Instead, segment your money; find different places to put it so you won't be tempted to misuse it or create a situation where money for different purposes is confused in a common account. This will help you to keep your financial affairs in order and allow you to monitor your progress in different savings categories.

Step 7. Streamline Your Financial Affairs

Many savings and investment products allow you to make automatic deposits into your accounts. This is an ideal way to make regular monthly payments without having to mail in a check or make a deposit. It is also a convenient way of saving, since the money is withdrawn from your account before you even realize it is there.

Similarly, many savings programs often allow you to have money withheld from your paycheck and directed toward savings accounts. By using such an approach, you routinely reserve money for yourself before you get your hands on your paycheck. This automatic withdrawal off the top of your paycheck is an ideal means of "forced savings."

Another excellent way of streamlining your financial affairs is to utilize direct deposit. This allows you to designate specific recurring payments you receive to be deposited automatically

into your account on a regular basis. By arranging to have payments directly deposited, you receive funds more conveniently
and securely. And if your money is directly deposited into an
interest-bearing account or an investment product, your earnings start when your deposit is received, not when you finally
make it to your financial institution with your deposit.

You can also have bill payments made automatically as well.
This saves you the hassle of sitting down and writing out
monthly bill-payment checks every month. And because payments are made automatically, you are assured that your bills
get paid on time each month.

CHAPTER 3

Reviewing and Improving Your Credit Report

Barbara has been looking for a house for the past several years. She finally fell in love with something but discovered to her dismay that her lender wouldn't approve her mortgage application because her credit report was so bad. If she'd known about how bad it was, she would have taken steps to improve it over the past several years.

One thing is certain: all mortgage lenders are going to get a copy of and will carefully scrutinize your credit report. This very important document tells prospective lenders how you've repaid debts you've owed in the past. Most lenders heavily rely on the information found in credit reports. As a result, it's extremely important that you understand your credit report and take whatever steps necessary to improve or correct the information it contains. Rather than being put in the position of having to "explain away" problems a potential mortgage lender discovers on your credit report, it's best to clean up your credit report as much as possible before a lender sees it.

A review of your credit history might well reveal inaccurate or incomplete information. If this is the case, with a few simple steps you may be able to clear up your credit rating and restore your creditworthiness. For example, you may have paid off one of your creditors, but your credit report still reflects a substantial balance due. As a result, a prospective lender may view you as overextended. By revising the balance-due figure to reflect your current zero balance, you are strengthening your credit report. Similarly, you might be able to minimize the damage of any unfavorable information that is being reported through the inclusion of a personal statement explaining the reasons.

What Are Credit-Reporting Agencies?

Credit-reporting agencies (also commonly referred to as credit bureaus) gather, store, and disseminate information relating to the identity, paying habits, and financial well-being of individuals. This information is obtained from creditors who routinely report such information to credit-reporting agencies and from public information available through court records and other public documents.

The role of credit-reporting agencies is to provide creditors with information concerning your creditworthiness. They serve merely as a source or library of information concerning your financial well-being. These agencies provide information concerning your past performance, which can then be used as a predictor of future performance by potential creditors. They do not decide whether your credit application should be accepted or denied. Rather, based on information provided by credit-reporting agencies, prospective creditors, applying their own credit-granting criteria, determine the fate of your credit application.

Since credit-reporting agencies maintain credit reports on millions of people, they are highly automated facilities, with most activities occurring through computerized transmittals.

Which Credit-Reporting Agencies Maintain Reports on You?

More than one credit-reporting agency may be maintaining a report on you. Since these agencies maintain separate, independent reports, clearing up a problem with one agency has *no* effect on how this same information may be reported by another.

Ask prospective lenders or other financial institutions for the names and addresses of the credit-reporting agencies that serve your local area. You can also check with your local chamber of commerce, better business bureau, or retail merchants association (if one exists in your local area). Or, contact the four largest credit-reporting agencies, at the addresses below, to determine if they maintain a report on you:

TRW Credit Data
505 City Parkway West, Suite 110
Orange, CA 92613-5450
714-991-6000

The Credit Bureau, Inc.
(also known as CBI/Equifax)
5501 Peachtree Dunwoody Road, Suite 600
Atlanta, GA 30356
404-250-4000

Trans Union Credit Information Company
444 North Michigan Avenue
Chicago, IL 60611
312-645-0012

CSC Credit Services, Inc.
652 East North Belt, Suite 133
Houston, TX 77060
713-878-4840

The above are the headquarters addresses of these companies. Your request will probably be referred to the regional office that maintains reports for your local area. Since the above telephone numbers access busy, computerized switchboards, it is probably best to make your request in writing, saving yourself long-distance telephone charges.

A look at your local yellow pages (in a rural area, the yellow pages of the largest city near you) under "Credit Reporting

Agencies" will also probably reveal the names of several agencies that serve your area. Some of these will be smaller firms that maintain local or regional reports; others may be the major agencies. Beware: some of the firms listed in the yellow pages may be limited in scope (for example, they may provide only mortgage-related credit information). Thus, if you use the yellow pages, be on the lookout for the names of the major credit-reporting agencies above, or ask, when you call, if the agencies compile comprehensive consumer-credit information. Once you have found a credit-reporting agency that maintains a report on you, you might also ask them for the names of other credit-reporting agencies that are likely to have your credit history on file.

What Information Is Contained in Your Credit Report?

Credit reports contain information about the types of credit accounts you have; your past and present repayment activities on loans, charge accounts, credit cards, and other extensions of credit; and whether you have ever filed bankruptcy or been sued. However, since some creditors do not report, or may only report certain accounts (that is, delinquent accounts), to credit-reporting agencies, some of your accounts may *not* appear on your credit report.

In addition, any current accounts you have will remain on your credit report indefinitely. These include your revolving charge cards, credit cards, open-end loans, or lines of credit.

Adverse Information

Credit-reporting agencies are prohibited from reporting adverse information beyond certain prescribed time periods. The following types of information can be reported only for the indicated periods:

Delinquent accounts, accounts placed for collection, accounts charged to profit and loss or as bad debts by creditors, court judgments = 7 years

Bankruptcies = 10 years

Your Right to Review Your Credit Report

Everyone has the right to review his or her own credit report. Upon request and with proper identification, every credit-reporting agency must clearly and accurately disclose to the consumer:

- The nature and substance of all information in its reports on the consumer at the time of the request

- The sources of the information

- The recipients of any credit-related consumer report it has furnished during the last six months

Costs of Credit Reports

If you have been declined credit within the last thirty days, the credit-reporting agency that provided your prospective creditor a copy of your credit report must disclose to you *without charge* the contents of this report. The identity of the credit-reporting agency that furnished this information should be clearly indicated on the rejection letter from your creditor.

If you have *not* been declined credit within the last thirty days, you may still review the contents of your credit report, provided you pay a fee. Costs range from five to twenty dollars, depending on the credit-reporting agency and the state in which you live.

Reviewing Your Credit Report

To enable you to evaluate the contents of your credit report, make every effort to obtain a written copy. Most major credit-reporting agencies currently provide written copies of credit reports to consumers. In addition, some state laws require the written disclosure of credit-report information. However, federal law does *not* require these consumer disclosures to be made in writing.

You may review the contents of your credit report via one of the following three methods:

- *In person.* A person may review his or her credit report at the consumer-reporting agency during normal business hours and on reasonable notice, provided proper identification is furnished. Make an appointment and bring the required information.

- *By telephone.* Before telephone disclosure can occur, you must first make a written request, with proper identification. In addition, you are responsible for any telephone charges incurred. Often, recorded messages, busy signals, and long hold periods make this the least desirable way of dealing with a credit-reporting agency.

- *By mail.* If you have been declined credit within the past thirty days, send a copy of your creditor's rejection letter to the appropriate credit-reporting agency. Indicate that you want a copy of your credit report. Make sure that you include all pertinent information (like your current mailing address and Social Security number). Also, be sure to sign your request.

Understanding Your Credit Report

Once your credit report has been disclosed to you, if you are unfamiliar with computer printouts and/or with deciphering credit reports, you may have your work cut out for you. Credit reports can be very difficult to understand.

Often provided on computer paper, these reports are usually cluttered with symbols and abbreviations that are meaningless to the uninitiated reader. Your best bet is to wade through the explanatory information that accompanies your credit report. Get a magnifying glass if you must, but it is well worth your while to understand, and gain a basic familiarity with, the contents of your credit report.

Credit-reporting agencies are required to provide trained personnel to explain any information contained in your credit report. Therefore, if there is something you do not understand, do not hesitate to ask for help.

In addition, you are entitled to bring a person of your choosing to help you decipher your credit report. Try to bring someone who is trustworthy and will respect the confidentiality of the information. If you can find somebody who is knowledgeable about credit reports, that would obviously be helpful. Whomever you choose to bring, make sure he or she comes armed with identification, since it will probably be required by the credit-reporting agency. The agency may also require you to furnish a written statement granting permission to discuss your report in another person's presence.

When reviewing your credit report, take time to evaluate each entry. Jot down all adverse information as well as any information you feel is incorrect or incomplete.

Things to Look Out for When Reviewing Your Credit History

When carefully reviewing your credit report, make certain all the information is accurate. Correct any incorrect background information—such as current and past employment, address information, and salary figures. In addition, pay particular attention to the following key categories appearing on the report. Make sure that:

All accounts listed on your credit report are yours. Sometimes, due to name similarities and other factors, it is possible for an account to be incorrectly reported on someone else's credit report.

All outstanding balances are accurate. It could be that a particular account has been paid in full, yet is reflected on your credit report as an amount still outstanding. This might make you appear to be overextended to any future creditors who review your credit report.

All past-due amounts are correct. If all of your accounts are current, no past-due amounts should be reflected.

All dates of last activity or status dates are correct. This is especially important on accounts that carry a negative rating, since these accounts will remain on your credit report for seven years from the date of last activity. This date could be the date of your most recent or final payment, date the account was referred to an outside collection agency, date the account was written off by the creditor, date a judgment was obtained, and so on.

There are no duplicate submissions. Sometimes the same amount will be reported twice on your credit report. This is called a "duplicate submission." Sometimes account numbers may be transposed or contain minor variations. As a result, the same account may appear on your credit report more than once. When questioning such duplicate submissions, you should indicate which submission you consider to be the more accurate.

All court or public records indicated are accurate.   If you question the validity of this type of entry, you will have to petition the court of appropriate jurisdiction before the entry can be removed from your credit report.

All account-status reports are accurate.   Since these status designations reflect your payment history for each account, they are the most important information contained in your credit report. These designations serve as the primary basis on which a creditor will either grant or deny you credit.

Improving Your Credit Report

The best way to develop a solid credit report is to pay your bills in a timely fashion, according to the terms of your loan or account agreements. However, even though you may have a stellar repayment history, a review of your credit report may reveal obligations that you feel are inaccurate or incomplete. By following the recommendations below, you can have a substantial impact on the way such obligations are reported on your credit report. To maximize your input in the contents of your credit report, you must:

- Preserve your rights under the Federal Fair Credit Reporting Act.
- Contact your creditors directly.

Do not expect to clear up your credit report overnight. Correcting incomplete or inaccurate credit-report information often takes several weeks or months. Just be patient and persistent.

Preserving Your Rights Under the Fair Credit Reporting Act

The federal Fair Credit Reporting Act (FCRA) protects your privacy concerning your credit obligations. It also gives you specific rights designed to assure the maximum possible accuracy of items contained in your credit report. It is a self-help law that allows you to challenge the accuracy or completeness of credit-report entries.

The act provides a mechanism for correcting *erroneous* information in your credit report. It does *not* allow you to have an accurately reported negative credit history erased.

To assure the accuracy or completeness of items contained in your credit report, take a critical look at all items reflected in it. Assert your rights about any items with which you disagree or that you believe should be more fully explained.

Disputing credit report information. If you wish to dispute the accuracy or completeness of information contained in your credit report, indicate all such items either on the dispute form or in the spaces provided on the credit report itself. Try to keep these disputes as brief and concise as possible.

You must challenge the accuracy or completeness of items that are currently reflected on your credit report. You cannot argue incompleteness just because an obligation does not appear on your credit report. Rather, you must take issue with the way particular items that currently appear on your credit report *are* reported.

In addition, your dispute must actually challenge the accuracy or completeness of the item of information in your credit report relating to the debt. You cannot merely provide a reason for payment problems—such as the death of a spouse, an illness, the loss of a job, and so on. Rather, your dispute must specifically relate to the information actually being reported. For example, if another person's account is reflected on your credit report, your dispute must address the accuracy of this entry.

After you have written down all of your disputes, submit them to the credit-reporting agency. Keep a copy for your records, making sure to note the date on which they were mailed.

Credit-reporting agencies must reinvestigate disputed information. By disputing information in your report, you shift the burden for continued inclusion of the information to the credit-reporting agency and the original creditor. Credit-reporting agencies are required to follow reasonable procedures to assure the maximum possible accuracy of information in their reports. The credit-reporting agency must reinvestigate and record the current status of disputed information within a reasonable period of time (thirty days) after receiving your dispute.

To conduct its reinvestigation, the credit-reporting agency will contact the original creditor, advise him or her of your dispute, and state your position. The original creditor will then be asked to confirm the information, qualify it, or accept your explanation.

If the original creditor fails to respond to the credit-reporting agency within a reasonable period of time, the disputed information will be deleted from your report, since it can no longer be verified. Similarly, if the creditor accepts your explanation, the disputed information will either be deleted or revised to reflect a more accurate status. However, if the original creditor confirms or qualifies the information, such information or revised information will continue to appear on your credit report.

Your right to a statement. If the reinvestigation does not resolve your dispute, you may file a brief statement, for inclusion in your credit report, describing the nature of your dispute. Then, in any subsequent reports containing the adverse information, the credit-reporting agency must clearly note that the information is disputed and provide either your statement or a clear and accurate summary thereof.

If you file a statement, it must relate to the obligation in question and not merely explain extenuating circumstances or present a rationalization for payment problems. In addition, the credit-reporting agency may limit your statement to one hundred words (for each disputed item) if it provides you with assistance in writing a clear summary of the dispute.

Your statement should be positive and upbeat. Rather than slamming the creditor with disparaging comments, accentuate your positive actions, like taking responsibility for resolving a difficult matter. The following example demonstrates this point:

> This obligation was paid off under a repayment plan voluntarily entered into and mutually agreeable to both parties. Final payment was made on _____, three months earlier than required under the payment plan. The creditor has since reinstated the account, which is now current.

Preparing a statement for inclusion in your credit report affords you the opportunity to tell your side of the story. Thus, creditors will be able to consider your statement alongside the adverse entry.

Contacting Your Creditors Directly

The above describes how you can dispute items contained in your credit report using the framework specifically provided under the Fair Credit Reporting Act. However, you should also contact all creditors with whom you have a dispute to see if the matter can be resolved directly. Make certain all such communications with creditors are in writing.

Directly contacting your creditors demonstrates your sincerity in wanting to get the matter resolved and personalizes your creditors' frame of reference for you. In addition, since many creditors are computerized, some items must be removed at the source so they will not continue to be reported with the creditor's regular transmittals to credit-reporting agencies.

When contacting your creditors, advise them you have

become aware of adverse information they are currently reporting on your credit report. Tell them you feel this information is either inaccurate or incomplete. Explain your version of account activities, providing enough information so that creditors have some logical basis for giving you the benefit of the doubt and granting your request. Suggest solutions you feel would more accurately reflect the status of your account.

CHAPTER 4

Shopping for a Mortgage

Lisa and Keith spent a year and a half hunting for the home of their dreams. They finally found it and were anxious to get their mortgage and move in. When they picked up the local Sunday newspaper and found a listing of mortgage rates available in their area, they were intimidated by all of the complex and confusing information provided and didn't really know where to start.

Finding the right mortgage depends on a number of factors and requires a thorough evaluation of the benefits, drawbacks, and special requirements of each type of mortgage. You need to ask yourself several basic questions as a prospective buyer selecting a mortgage loan. First, you should consider how quickly you would like to repay the loan. Most loans require that the loan be paid off in 15, 20, or 30 years. Typically, the sooner you repay the loan, the more money you save in interest payments. The longer the term of the loan, the lower the monthly payments are. You should also consider how long you plan to live in the home you are buying, and the monthly payment amount that you can safely handle. Like any other consumer purchase that you make, it is important that you shop around for the loan that not only offers the best deal but also best corresponds to your present and future financial and personal needs.

Your mortgage is probably the single most expensive item you will ever buy. That's right—your mortgage, not your house.

You will spend far more in interest for your house than you will pay for your house! A $100,000 mortgage at 8 percent over 30 years will cost you $164,240 in interest—more than one and a half times the cost of the house. As much as you may hate shopping, "shop till you drop" before you complete an application.

Mortgage-pricing terms have a tremendous impact upon the ultimate cost of your mortgage. Consider the difference one percent interest can make over the life of the mortgage. Payments for a $100,000 mortgage for 30 years are $805/month at 9 percent and $734/month at 8 percent, a $71 difference. The difference is $25,560 over the 30-year life of the mortgage. But if you had found an 8 percent mortgage and had put the difference—$71 every month for thirty years into a conservative mutual fund 30 years ago—you would have $174,213 cash toward your retirement plus your house. The real cost of money is not in saving $25,560, but what that saving could have bought.

In a recent "mystery shopper" test of ten lenders for standard fixed-rate or adjustable-rate mortgages (conventional loans) in a major city, the shoppers found:

- A difference of one percentage point in fixed-rate mortgage interest rates (after adjusting for varying point charges, introductory rates, etc.)

- A three-point spread in adjustable-rate mortgages' (ARMs) starting interest rate (after adjusting for varying point charges, etc.)

- Considerable "steering" toward ARMs, which adjusted interest rates every 6 months or yearly

- A range of 3–20% in the amount of down payment required

- 97% loans that didn't require private mortgage insurance (PMI)

- A range of 0 to 2 points charged at closing

- A few lenders with special programs that provided better than market interest rates, no points, and rebates on closing costs for buyers with credit problems

Obviously there are tremendous differences in what's available from different lenders even in the same area. These mystery shoppers went to one or two lenders who advertised an 8 percent annual rate, and if the lender found the shoppers' debts to be a little higher than their normal standard or a few credit problems—no problem. They had a special home-buyer program for our mystery shopper at a lower interest rate, no points, and a $600 rebate on their closing costs. Congratulations, you've just hit the jackpot!

The same mystery shoppers with the same house and the exact same financial characteristics went to several other lenders with the same advertised rate. However, since their debts were a little high (or even if they weren't high, but the lender just happened to err and calculate them on the high side), they were urged to take a different loan with higher interest rates. Or, more typically, they were steered to ARMs. They were told that the only loan they could qualify for was an ARM, often a forty-year ARM, which is very lucrative to the lender. Too bad, you've just been taken to the cleaners!

How do you know if you are likely to hit the jackpot or be taken to the cleaners? There is no way to know unless you shop around. Will you know by the type of financial institution— bank, savings association, mortgage company, credit association, or finance company? No. Will the size of their facilities, the charm and knowledge of their employees, give you a clue? No. Will you know by whether they come to you or you go to them? No. Irrespective of your proficiency with financial issues, the appealing loan offer you may have received, who recommended you (including your realtor, your pastor, a friend, or a housing-counseling service), one constant remains. Check out the competition.

Ironically, many people spend months or years looking for a house and agonizing over whether they should take the big plunge into home ownership. After all of this they often rush to closure on the first mortgage they find. Or work with only one broker because he/she is so nice and "comes to my house or office." Tragically, they do not even check with others. But perseverance pays.

Never forget the mortgage hunter's credo: shop, shop, shop, shop, shop. After following the advice offered in Chapter 1 on avoiding pitfalls, seize the bull by the horns. Go out and find the absolute best mortgage deal available, one that specifically suits your needs. Start with advice from family, friends, colleagues, realtor, pastor—everyone who thinks they have a good lead or person. Ask your realtor if they have a computerized mortgage database. Large realtors generally have loan information from many firms. Scanning a computerized database should be free or very inexpensive.

Then let your fingers do the walking under "mortgages" in the yellow pages. This will include banks, savings associations, and mortgage companies. If the list is too long, focus on those who advertise. Avoid those who suggest that they have a loan for "everyone." Check with your employer, union, credit union, church, etc.—they may have a relationship with a lender that includes mortgages for members/employees. Take a day or two to do your preliminary shopping—that is not much time to spend on the most expensive item you are likely to buy.

You also need to insulate yourself emotionally. Being told you do not qualify for a loan is a pretty devastating experience. Being told over and over again can be severe punishment. If you can, look at it as gamesmanship—pretend you are doing the research for a friend. Pretend your boss gave you an assignment or your friend asked you to do him/her a favor. In other words, take yourself and your feelings out of the equation. Know that in your marketplace there are a few jackpots and that, with perseverance, you will find them! Keep a cool, independent attitude. Don't allow yourself to be "sold" by a sympathetic loan officer, to change your goal, or to be diverted.

Check current prices by phone with dozens of lenders. Compare this to any listings in your local newspaper. This will give you a benchmark figure. If you have negotiated and signed a sales contract on a house already, it's probably not a bad idea to drop in on the ten best mortgage lenders you find. They should be willing to take you without an appointment if you have a signed contract in hand. If you don't have a contract in hand, call first. Tell the lender you are shopping for a house and a mortgage simultaneously. Pick a likely house price. If they won't see you without a contract, find another lender who is willing to work with you at your own pace.

If you're told that you do not qualify for the best rate available at the time you are shopping, ask the lender about the availability of any special programs. If the lender seems intent on pushing a particular product, bear in mind that the whole purpose of this exercise is to find what's best for you, not to satisfy a lender's desire to maximize profits—at your expense. For example, if a particular lender seems intent on selling you an ARM when you want fixed-rate, or if they suggest a more expensive fixed-rate loan than you had expected, get the information and leave. Then go to a lender who listens to your needs and is willing to work within the parameters you have established. Also, don't give up on getting a market-priced mortgage until you've contacted or analyzed what is available from at least ten different lenders.

If you keep encountering the same seemingly insurmountable problems from every lender you contact, it may be wise to put off buying a house for a little while to get your ducks in a row and fix whatever problems have been identified. For example, if you have too much debt, you may need to bring your indebtedness within tolerable limits before you'll be able to qualify for a mortgage on favorable terms or to get one at all. In such cases, you might consider working with a nonprofit housing-counseling agency in order to get a competitive-rate mortgage. Many counseling organizations have agreements with lenders that go into effect with only six to twelve months of credit repair (instead of the more traditional three to seven years). Ask about their relationships with lenders before you select a counseling agency. If you have to have a mortgage now and are prepared to pay a premium interest rate, the counselors will refer you to a lender with a relatively low interest rate for your situation. However, check out those yourself as well.

You really do need to protect yourself for a variety of reasons. With so much competition out there and lenders competing for your business, you should be able to find the right mortgage on the best available terms. Even though you may have been through the mortgage process before when you purchased another home, the marketplace has changed dramatically in recent years. New products are available that weren't in existence only a couple of years ago. What's more, most people buy very few mortgages in their lifetimes. Since mortgage issues are so complex and confusing, it's very easy to be intimidated by a seemingly reputable lender who may take you for a ride if you're not careful. It's in your best interest to be on your toes even with the most reputable lenders to protect yourself and possibly shave costs off your mortgage.

Mortgages generate significant up-front income for brokers, loan officers, and others involved in the mortgage process. The broker or loan officer gets paid, upon closing, based on the cost of the mortgage and the type of the mortgage. Then, the lender sells the mortgage to the secondary market and makes its money up front as well. The lender's income is also based on the amount, type (fixed or ARM), length, interest rate of the loan, and the points charged. So, if the lender can stick you with a higher interest rate on an ARM, that product can be sold more readily by the lender in the secondary market than a lower-rate fixed mortgage. Thus, the amount of profit that the lender and the loan officer or mortgage broker make is based on the type of loan that they sell you. The higher the amount, interest rate, length of loan, points, etc., the more money they both make. Understanding this financial relationship should help you understand why some lenders work so hard to sell you something that you may not want. Or, why some lenders charge a little (or a lot) more when they can get away with it.

While your mortgage represents a long-term investment on your part, the mortgage-lending industry is not necessarily based on long-term relationships. That's because your loan will likely be sold to another lender shortly after it's made. As a result, you may wind up mailing your monthly payment to an address in another part of the country. Or, to someone other than your original lender. You may not even realize that your mortgage payment is going to a financial entity you may have never heard of. But don't despair. Such circumstances represent business as usual in the mortgage industry. The terms and conditions of your mortgage will not change even though the mortgage itself changes hands.

In addition to large companies that make loans using their own loan officers, there are independent mortgage brokers. Some of these are worth their weight in gold. They have contacts with many lenders, know the loans and the qualifications, know how to make you look good as an applicant, and can serve you well (at a nominal charge). They, ideally, would do for you what you haven't the time to do—shop for a loan. However, even there you must be wary and do some checking for yourself. A mortgage broker serves you best when you do the initial shopping, set a target rate for your mortgage, and have several brokers see how close and how well they can come toward meeting that rate. You then go with the best.

But, remember, lenders tempt mortgage brokers with all kinds of bonus money if they can bring in a loan that is above market rate or an ARM. It is very hard today to know whom the broker is working for. You will only know if your needs are met if you first set your own goals for your mortgage.

There is no one out there but you to watch out for your interests. Lenders are fighting for their own survival in a highly competitive market. Many are waiting to pounce on the next likely candidate for a mortgage who'll make them some money. And if they think you do not know much about mortgages, they will gladly sell you one on more expensive terms than you may have been able to obtain.

Whatever loan you are applying for—make sure that the lender does that loan type frequently. For example, if you decide on an FHA or VA loan, do not go to a lender that does five or six of these a year, but a lender who specializes in these special types of loans (also known as a direct endorsement lender). The same thing is true for special programs. If you're interested in a particular type of loan, ask the lender how many loans of this specific type they do a year. Lenders may offer to do something they don't do very well. Since your mortgage is so important to your financial future, don't let them test the waters with you. You may not be well served in this instance.

The same is true of the person who interviews you. When you make an appointment, ask for an experienced loan officer. If you get an officer who is new and inexperienced, or if they say that this is their first week or month, that they don't do much with mortgages, or offer any other clue that they don't really know what they are doing, don't waste your time! If you are already into the interview, make it short. Try again at another location, or make an appointment and ask for an experienced person. This is your loan—while you care about others' feelings, you must first protect yourself!

A Tale of Three Mortgage Seekers

The following identifies three different types of borrowers and the types of loans they were able to obtain which suited their needs. Obviously, your individual circumstances will vary. But these examples illustrate the kinds of issues you'll undoubtedly encounter as you shop around.

John.   In his early twenties John was a fast-food manager. He spent his money as fast as, or even before, he made it. Since he was spending over $1,000 a month in rent, his parents suggested he consider buying a place. He found the right house and applied for a 15-year FHA mortgage, since he had little savings (only a 3 percent down payment is required) and he had a lot of debt (FHA permits a debt ratio of 41 percent). He was also able to use a gift letter from his parents to qualify. He wound up getting a 15-year loan instead of a 30-year loan because his income was high enough to support the loan. Making mortgage payments was also a way of "enforced savings," which enabled him to sock away money before he could spend it. What's more, if the money didn't go into the house, John would probably spend rather than save.

John began complaining in the early years about his high payments. Life would be more fun if he paid less each month, and he talked about refinancing to a 30-year loan. Since interest rates had gone down, he wanted to refinance to a lower rate and a longer term. But John's credit-card lifestyle had caught up with him, and he could not qualify for a lower rate loan because of his high debt ratio. Thus, he was stuck with his 15-year, higher-rate mortgage.

Five years later, John is not only more mature, but a happy man. He has only ten years to go on his mortgage. He is well along his way toward paying off his high debts. He now owns his own restaurant and used his house as collateral for a bank loan to open his business. While he plans to move up to a bigger house someday, owning this house free and clear in ten years now sounds great, and he plans to use it as rental income.

Joe and Jodi.   Joe and his wife, Jodi, young professionals, always made sure to have money in the bank. When they bought their first house, they knew it would not be the only house they'd ever buy. Since they were both collectors and planned on raising a family someday, they knew they'd be in their first house for no more than five years. In the meantime, their incomes as well as their savings would grow. In addition, both were analytical, loved financial challenges, and were involved in finances in their respective jobs. They worked with mortgage brokers to find the deals—but they knew what they were looking for and understood the need to take responsibility for what they get and to negotiate. Joe says, "It's just like buying a car—you would never accept the given price on a car. Why on earth would you ever consider doing that on a mortgage?"

At this time, a good rate for a 30-year fixed mortgage in their area was 9 percent. They started with a 30-year ARM which was fixed at 7 percent for the first 3 years (an ARM fixed for the first 3 years of a 30-year term is often referred to as a "3/30" ARM). They figured they would come out ahead, with only one rise in interest rates before they were out of this house. They also put 20 percent down, borrowing half of that as a second mortgage from another lender at a fixed rate of 10 percent for 15 years. This eliminated the need for PMI, and since they were good savers, they made extra payments when they could to build equity on this second.

After four years in the house, however, mortgage rates on fixed-rate loans dropped to 7 percent in their area. After making dozens of phone calls, they found a lender who would refinance without points. Thus, for only $500 they refinanced, cut their monthly payments, and even got some cash back. The $500 refinancing fee was "paid off" in savings in a few months.

A year later, they bought a bigger house, paid 3 points to get a 6 ¾ percent (compared to 7 ½ percent at the time), 30-year fixed mortgage for a house they'll live in for quite some time. They called several mortgage brokers, told them what they were looking for, and went with the broker who could deliver the best deal. Their 3 points will be "paid off" in savings on monthly payments over five years—after that it is as if they never paid the points.

Bear in mind one important caveat for someone who wants to play the system the way that Jim and Jodi were able to do. These mortgage gymnastics are normally possible only when you have salaried, long-term jobs and perfect credit. If Joe or Jodi had lost their job, or if they were not diligent in keeping substantial savings to cover that occurrence, they could have been "stuck" in any one of their positions. Taking temporary loans, like an ARM, should be done only by persons with very strong financial situations (either income, savings, and/or sources of financial help from family). An ARM should never be taken just because you cannot afford a fixed-rate mortgage.

Jillean. Jillean, an artist and part-time framer, had the hardest time getting a mortgage even though she had a very large down payment and perfect credit. This was because some of her income would come from her sale of art and some from rental of rooms in her house. Because of her decision to pursue her art, Jillean knew her income would likely be limited over her lifetime. She also didn't want any financial surprises and had no interest in second-guessing the financial markets. She wanted the smallest possible fixed payment. She decided to try to get a 30-year fixed conventional mortgage. Despite many rejections and the discouragement of her realtor, Jillean got just the loan she was looking for from a bank. She took the advice of a friend who told her to get a letter from her employer of many years saying that Jillean was: due to get a raise next month; had worked for her for many years; was a wonderful worker; and the employer was offering her a full-time job. That letter helped her get the loan she wanted.

Today, Jillean works part-time as a framer, paints in her home studio, rents two rooms in her house, and makes her monthly payments on her mortgage—happily knowing that except for small increases in property taxes, the payments will always be the same.

CHAPTER 5

Getting Started

Ray and Kim's lease expires soon, and they may not be allowed to renew. If they have to move, Ray wonders if they should buy this time. Kim thinks a house will be too expensive. Kim's friend Alan thinks that interest rates will stay low and that with the tax advantages, owning a house will be cheaper than renting.

Comparing the Costs of Home Ownership and Renting

People buy homes for many reasons. These include investment, the security and pride of owning your own home, the chance to own your home free and clear during your retirement, and, often, for household budgetary savings resulting from the mortgage-interest deduction. Some of these reasons have emotional value, and others have dollar values. All of these reasons are valid, and their cumulative value will determine if home ownership makes sense for you.

While this chapter cannot help you determine the value of the emotional advantages/disadvantages of home ownership, the following calculations will provide a framework and checklist for estimating the cost of ownership compared to the cost of renting. Comparative costs over the first year as well as the long-term costs are evaluated. These projections are highly individual, but should include:

- Major maintenance costs

- Appreciation/Depreciation

- Forgone interest on down payment and closing costs

- Forgone interest on mortgage payments in excess of potential rent payments

- Sale costs (including real estate commission and spruce-up costs)

- Property tax increases

In the following discussions, examples provide sample numbers for calculations.

Mortgage Payment Calculation

After you decide on the term you wish to repay the mortgage over (typically thirty years), look up the current lending rates available (call several lenders or check the Sunday paper). After you determine the interest rate you will have to pay:

1. Consult the table in this chapter for the payment amount (per thousand) per month you will make
2. Divide the principal amount you will borrow by $1,000 (e.g., for Len, below, this will be $300,000/$1,000 = 300)
3. Multiply the amount per thousand (from step 1) by the number of thousands you will borrow (from step 2) for your total payment per month

Len wants a house of his own that he doesn't have to share with anyone else (there are too many parties where he lives now). He currently earns $120,000 a year. He has found the house he wants, and the woman who owns it will either give him a long-term lease at $2,300 a month or sell him the house for $350,000. Len has $50,000 saved from a book he wrote and can use this for a down payment, requiring a mortgage of $300,000. He has checked with a bank and can get a 30-year fixed interest rate of 8 *percent. The $50,000 dollars he has saved is currently earning 5 percent interest. Len also asked Kim's friend Alan about interest rates, and Alan thinks that 5 percent is about all he'll get for the next few years.)*

For Len these calculations will be:

Term: 30 years
Interest Rate: 8%
Principal $300,000
Principal divided by $1,000   300
Payment per $1,000 per month $7.34/mo.
Monthly payment calculation $7.34 × 300 = $2,201
Total yearly mortgage payments $26,416

Mortgage Interest Tax-Deduction Calculation

You save money on your federal income tax payment when you own a home (see Chapter 14 for detailed tax information). The amount you save is dependent on two numbers, which change over the course of your mortgage, (1) your "tax bracket," and (2) the amount of your yearly payment that is interest rather than principal repayment. To calculate how much you will save on income tax payment through the mortgage interest deduction, do the following:

1. Estimate your current tax bracket (see task 1 in the calculation worksheet in Chapter 14) and your tax bracket in the next several years (you may use your tax bracket from last year if your income and deductions will not change substantially and if the tax code has not changed)
2. Calculate the mortgage interest you will pay per year (ask your mortgage lender to calculate the interest payment amount you will pay in the 1st, 5th, 10th, 15th, 20th, and 25th years)
3. Multiply your yearly mortgage interest payment by your tax bracket.

The number that results will be your annual federal tax savings. For Len, these calculations will be:

Tax bracket:	31%
Monthly payments (30-Year, $300,000 Mortgage at 8%):	$2,201
Yearly payments	$26,416

Interest Deduction Calculations:

	Interest Payment (Interest Deduction)	Tax Saving (Initial Payment × 31%)
Year 1	$23,909	$7,412
5	22,969	7,120
10	21,280	6,597
15	18,764	5,817
20	11,401	3,534
25	9,431	2,924
30	0	0

Cost of Owning Versus Renting

Once you have calculated your mortgage payment and the tax savings ownership will provide, you are ready to compare ownership and rental costs. There are a number of expenses and benefits to consider in the comparison. A checklist for these expenses is:

OWNING

Costs:

- Yearly mortgage
- Forgone interest on down payment
- Closing costs
- Forgone interest on closing costs

- Property taxes
- Maintenance costs
- Property and liability insurance
- Utilities
- Potential depreciation in the property's value

Benefits:

- Tax savings from mortgage
- Equity accumulation
- Potential appreciation in the property's value

RENTING

Costs:

- Yearly rent payments
- Maintenance (yard only)
- Utilities

To compare the costs fully, you must identify each of the above items. Moreover, you will need to calculate the costs for various years, since rental costs will go up and the tax savings from the interest deduction will go down. Because no one really knows what will happen to costs in future years, make your best guess for your calculations. A 3–5 percent yearly inflation rate is a safe assumption for long-term projections; there is no safe assumption for appreciation/depreciation.

When Len sits down to figure out whether he should buy, his calculations are the following:

Tax Implications of Renting

Income	$120,000
Interest from $50,000 savings	2,500
Gross income	122,500
Federal income taxes at 31%	37,975

Tax Implications of Owning
(using $50,000 for down payment)

Total mortgage payments ($2,201/mo.)	26,416
Mortgage interest for 1 year (payments − principal)	23,909
Property tax deduction (@ 1.25% of house value)	4,375
Gross income	120,000
Taxable income	91,717
[gross income − (mortgage interest + property tax deduction)]	
Federal income taxes at 31%	28,432
Tax Savings by Owning ($37,975 − $28,432)	$9,543

Costs of Owning (first year)

Yearly mortgage payments $2,201/mo. at 8%)	−26,416
Forgone interest on $50,000 down payment	−2,500
Closing costs ($4,000 amortized over 10 years)	−400
Foregone interest on closing costs (@ 5% yr.)	−200
Property taxes (at 1.25% of house value)	−4,305
Maintenance cost (interior, exterior, mechanical, yard)	−1,000
Property and liability insurance (estimated $1,000/year)	−1,000
Utilities (estimated $100/mo.)	−1,200
Tax savings from mortgage ($37,975 − $28,432)	+9,543
Equity earned (principal payment on mortgage)	+2,507
Total Cost of Owning for One Year	$24,971
(without credit/debit for house's appreciation/depreciation)	

Cost of Renting

Total rent payments (12 × $2,300/mo.)	−$27,600
Maintenance (yard only)	−200
Utilities	−1,000
Total Cost of Renting	$28,800
Savings if Owned (assuming no appreciation)	$3,829
Savings if Owned (assuming 1% appreciation) = $3500)	$7,329
Savings if Owned (assuming 3% appreciation) = $10,500)	$14,329
Savings if Rented* (assuming 3% depreciation)	$6,671

*$10,500 depreciation + $26,590 ownership cost less $28,800 rental cost)

The first year of home ownership seems to make sense for Len if home prices stay flat or appreciate. If home prices fall, however, short-term ownership does not look advantageous from a financial perspective. Unfortunately for Len, prices in Georgetown, where he wants to buy, have been falling for the last five years, and they don't appear to be stabilizing (the average home price in Georgetown fell 15 percent in 1995). In other areas of the country, however, appreciation is occurring.

As we can see with Len, many factors must be included in calculating whether owning or renting is more advantageous in terms of yearly costs. These examples should offer you a checklist and methodology for determining what is best in your situation.

What Size Mortgage Can You Afford?

Susan and Danny were anxious to buy a home. Still fairly young and decades away from their peak earning years, they wanted to buy as much home as they could afford without unduly strapping themselves for cash. They didn't want to wind up house poor.

To make absolutely certain you can afford a mortgage for homes of varying sizes, you need a ball park estimate of expected monthly mortgage payments. Using the Mortgage Payment Calculation Table below, you can calculate your approximate monthly payment for any fixed-rate mortgage at interest rates from 3 to 12.875 percent and with terms of 10, 15, 20, 25, or 30 years. The table's payments are calculated to amortize the mortgage payments evenly over the term of the mortgage, keeping your mortgage payments constant throughout the term of the mortgage. This means that your payment amount will not change during the term, despite the fact that the amount of principal and interest paid in each payment will shift over the life of the mortgage.

To use the table complete the following steps:

1. Choose the interest rate you expect to pay.
2. Find the column for the mortgage term you expect to use.
3. Find the dollar figure at the intersection of the interest rate row and the mortgage term column (this is the dollar amount you will pay every month for each thousand dollars of your mortgage principal).
4. Divide the mortgage amount you will request by 1,000.
5. Multiply the dollar figure from step 3 by the answer to step 4 (this will be your approximate monthly mortgage payment).

For example, if Susan and Danny expect to borrow $100,000 for 25 years at 8 percent, they look down the first column on the left side of the table to the 8 percent row. Next they find the 25-year column (fifth from the left) and look down it to where it intersects the 8 percent row. At the intersection they find the dollar figure of $7.72. They know that this figure is their monthly payment per thousand dollars of their mortgage, so they divide the $100,000 they plan to borrow by $1,000 to find the number they need to multiply $7.72 by. This calculation results in an answer of 100, telling them that they are borrowing 100 thousand-dollar increments. To finish their calculations, Susan and Danny multiply the $7.72 monthly payment per thousand by 100, finding that their total monthly payments for a $100,000 mortgage at 8 percent for 25 years will be approximately $772.00.

Mortgage Payment Calculation Table

Monthly Payment per $1,000 of Mortgage

(Interest Rate)	(Term)				
	10 years	15 years	20 years	25 years	30 years
3.000%	$9.65	$6.91	$5.55	$4.75	$4.22
3.125	9.71	6.97	5.62	4.82	4.29
3.250	9.77	7.03	5.68	4.88	4.36
3.375	9.83	7.09	5.74	4.95	4.43
3.500	9.89	7.15	5.80	5.01	4.50
3.625	9.95	7.22	5.87	5.08	4.57
3.750	10.01	7.28	5.93	5.15	4.64
3.875	10.07	7.34	6.00	5.21	4.71
4.000	10.13	7.40	6.06	5.28	4.78
4.125	10.19	7.46	6.13	5.35	4.85
4.250	10.25	7.53	6.20	5.42	4.92
4.375	10.31	7.59	6.26	5.49	4.99
4.500	10.37	7.65	6.33	5.56	5.07
4.625	10.43	7.72	6.40	5.63	5.14
4.750	10.49	7.78	6.47	5.71	5.22
4.875	10.55	7.85	6.54	5.78	5.29
5.000	10.61	7.91	6.60	5.85	5.37
5.125	10.67	7.98	6.67	5.92	5.44
5.250	10.73	8.04	6.74	6.00	5.53
5.375	10.80	8.11	6.81	6.07	5.60
5.500	10.86	8.18	6.88	6.15	5.68
5.625	10.92	8.24	6.95	6.22	5.76
5.750	10.98	8.31	7.03	6.30	5.84
5.875	11.04	8.38	7.10	6.37	5.92

(Interest Rate)			(Term)		
	10 years	15 years	20 years	25 years	30 years
6.000%	$11.11	$8.44	$7.17	$6.45	$6.00
6.125	11.17	8.51	7.24	6.52	6.08
6.250	11.23	8.58	7.31	6.60	6.16
6.375	11.30	8.65	7.39	6.68	6.24
6.500	11.36	8.72	7.46	6.76	6.33
6.625	11.42	8.78	7.53	6.84	6.40
6.750	11.49	8.85	7.61	6.91	6.49
6.875	11.55	8.92	7.68	6.99	6.57
7.000	11.62	8.99	7.76	7.07	6.65
7.125	11.68	9.06	7.83	7.15	6.74
7.250	11.75	9.13	7.91	7.23	6.82
7.375	11.81	9.20	7.98	7.31	6.91
7.500	11.88	9.28	8.06	7.39	6.99
7.625	11.94	9.35	8.14	7.48	7.08
7.750	12.01	9.42	8.21	7.56	7.16
7.875	12.07	9.49	8.29	7.64	7.25
8.000	12.14	9.56	8.37	7.72	7.34
8.125	12.20	9.63	8.45	7.81	7.43
8.250	12.27	9.71	8.53	7.89	7.52
8.375	12.34	9.78	8.60	7.97	7.61
8.500	12.40	9.85	8.68	8.06	7.69
8.625	12.47	9.93	8.76	8.14	7.78
8.750	12.54	10.00	8.84	8.23	7.87
8.875	12.61	10.07	8.92	8.31	7.96
9.000	12.67	10.15	9.00	8.40	8.05
9.125	12.74	10.22	9.08	8.48	8.14
9.250	12.81	10.30	9.16	8.57	8.23
9.375	12.88	10.37	9.24	8.66	8.32
9.500	12.94	10.45	9.33	8.74	8.41
9.625	13.01	10.52	9.41	8.83	8.50
9.750	13.08	10.60	9.49	8.92	8.59
9.875	13.15	10.67	9.57	9.00	8.69
10.000	13.22	10.75	9.66	9.09	8.78
10.125	13.29	10.83	9.74	9.18	8.87

(Interest Rate)			(Term)		
	10 years	15 years	20 years	25 years	30 years
10.250%	$13.36	$10.90	$9.82	$9.27	$8.97
10.375	13.43	10.98	9.90	9.36	9.06
10.500	13.50	11.06	9.99	9.45	9.15
10.625	13.57	11.14	10.07	9.54	9.25
10.750	13.64	11.21	10.16	9.63	9.34
10.875	13.71	11.29	10.24	9.72	9.43
11.000	13.78	11.37	10.33	9.81	9.53
11.125	13.85	11.45	10.41	9.90	9.62
11.250	13.92	11.53	10.50	9.99	9.72
11.375	13.99	11.61	10.58	10.08	9.81
11.500	14.07	11.69	10.67	10.17	9.91
11.625	14.14	11.77	10.76	10.26	10.00
11.750	14.21	11.85	10.84	10.36	10.10
11.875	14.28	11.93	10.93	10.44	10.20
12.000	14.35	12.01	11.02	10.54	10.29
12.125	14.42	12.09	11.10	10.63	10.39
12.250	14.49	12.17	11.19	10.72	10.48
12.375	14.56	12.25	11.28	10.82	10.58
12.500	14.63	12.33	11.37	10.92	10.68
12.625	14.70	12.41	11.46	11.02	10.78
12.750	14.77	12.49	11.55	11.12	10.88
12.875	14.84	12.57	12.66	11.22	10.98

Mortgage Pre-qualification

Theresa and Hank have been pre-qualified for a mortgage in the amount of $200,000 based upon their income and financial resources. As they look for a new home, they know exactly how much of a house and a monthly mortgage payment they can afford.

If you are seriously in the market for a home, you might consider "pre-qualifying" for a mortgage. Based upon your income, outstanding indebtedness, credit rating, and employment status, pre-qualification enables a mortgage lender to tell you just how much of a mortgage you can handle. With a pre-qualification letter in hand, you can dispense with seller and real estate agent questions about your economic status and how big a mortgage you can afford. Your pre-qualification approval, which is normally valid for a set number of days beyond the date on which it was issued, tells it all.

Increasing numbers of lenders will pre-qualify you in a process that takes anywhere from a couple of hours to a couple of days. By prequalifying, you can obtain advance approval for the maximum mortgage amount you can handle given your financial circumstances. In addition to telling you how much house you can handle, pre-qualification also tells you: how large a down payment you will need, how much money will be required at settlement, and the amount of the monthly payment if a mortgage of a certain amount is approved. This information can go a long way toward helping you appreciate the gravity of the expenditure you are contemplating. You can make certain to shop for houses in your price range and avoid looking at those above or below that mark.

Pre-qualification can also alert you to problems you may later experience with the mortgage application itself. For example, while prequalifying for a particular loan amount, your lender may discover potential problems with your credit report or income history. Because you still have the loan-application process ahead of you, you have the opportunity to correct problems before you reach major decision points in the mortgage-application process.

Some pre-qualifications are free if you ultimately write a mortgage contract with the lender who pre-qualifies you. Most can be done at minimal cost, usually for $50 or $60, which roughly approximates the lender's costs for obtaining copies of your credit reports. Most prequalifications do not result in any additional costs attached to your loan (i.e., pre-qualification should not wind up costing you a quarter or half of a point at the time of closing).

Pre-qualification does not confer upon you legal rights. It

does not ensure loan approval, nor does it lock you into an interest rate or other pricing components. Pre-qualification is simply the first step along the mortgage route. After pre-qualification you still must submit an application, provide the necessary documentation, and qualify for the loan.

Pre-qualification gives you a certain psychological advantage in the real estate marketplace. This is because pre-qualification proves to sellers and real estate agents that you are serious about wanting to purchase a home. Indeed, if you've persevered the hassles of providing personal financial information to a lender, you're probably more than a "tire kicker" in the eyes of real estate agents and sellers alike. This may come in handy if you're dealing with a seller who is anxious to unload his or her property and doesn't want to wait around for the normal three-month mortgage-qualification process. Pre-qualification shows that you are a reputable, serious contender.

Mortgage Pre-approval

Christopher has already applied for and been "pre-approved" for a mortgage in the amount of $80,000. Only problem is, he has not yet found the condo he wants to buy.

In contrast to mortgage pre-qualification, mortgage pre-approval confirms the actual amount a buyer can borrow in advance of a home purchase. To obtain pre-approval, home purchasers have to actually apply for and qualify for the mortgage. Once this happens, closing normally entails only property appraisals and sorting out the terms of the mortgage contract (i.e., interest rate, points, term, and monthly payment). Some lenders will even cap the interest rate on pre-approved loans for up to 270 days while buyers are out house hunting.

Like pre-qualification, pre-approval alerts the buyer, sellers, and real estate agents to how much house can be afforded. Since technical financial issues are dealt with up-front, needless hassles are avoided. Sellers know that prospective buyers have the financial wherewithal to sustain the mortgage. Buyers can avoid the worry of finding a home only to have their hopes dashed with a loan-application rejection and possible loss of their earnest-money deposit. On the up-side, if you've been pre-approved for a mortgage, you can negotiate like a cash buyer. Since you don't have the contingency of a loan rejection looming overhead, you can negotiate the best deal possible on your new place.

Unlike lock-ins (discussed later), pre-approval does not normally confer an exact interest rate, points, or other pricing components. These will all be determined at a later date. Pre-approval simply shows that you have qualified for a specific loan amount on terms yet to be determined.

CHAPTER 6

Different Types of Mortgages

Charles and Mary knew they wanted a mortgage with low monthly payments. But they weren't sure whether they should get a fixed- or adjustable-rate mortgage. Chris works hard but barely makes enough money to support his family. They've been living with his parents for some years now and would really love to find a home of their own. They could probably rent something, but the payments would be close to what they'd have to pay if they purchased a home.

For decades the only mortgage program in existence was the thirty-year fixed-rate loan. Today mortgage loans are offered at a variety of interest rates and terms. This means that more options are available to prospective home buyers. It also means that many people who previously would not have been able to qualify for a home loan may now become homeowners. Because of the many available options, however, it is more important than ever to understand the different types of mortgage loans before selecting the one that is best for you. This chapter identifies the various types of mortgages you'll encounter in today's marketplace.

As you shop around, you will undoubtedly find a host of mortgage lenders offering fixed- and adjustable-rate mortgages. Your first decision will probably be to determine which mortgage is right for you. You should also be aware of other types of loans and different loan programs for which you might qualify.

Fixed-Rate Mortgages

The conventional fixed-rate mortgage loan is one in which the monthly payments remain the same for as long as you have your loan. Fixed-rate loans cannot be altered by the lender or the borrower once the loan agreement has been signed. The interest rate charged does not fluctuate but remains constant throughout the length of the loan. The term *conventional* means that the loan is backed by a private lending institution instead of a government agency.

The fixed-rate loan is the most commonly used financing arrangement today. One of the greatest advantages of the fixed-rate loan is that it guarantees predictability for home buyers because the monthly payment never changes. The fixed-rate mortgage is often recommended for borrowers who are on a fixed monthly income and who want the certainty of knowing their payment amount each month. It is also a good option for people who plan to remain in their homes for several years or longer.

Also, if interest rates are low, you might opt for a fixed-rate loan that will lock you in to the best interest rate available on the loan date. If interest rates then go up or down, your interest rate will remain the same. You will be able to pay off your obligation at your contracted rate irrespective of changing economic conditions.

One drawback to the fixed-rate loan is that if interest rates decline below the fixed-interest rate of the loan, refinancing will be necessary in order to take advantage of the lower rates. The terms of the fixed-rate loan, as well as its down-payment requirements vary by lender.

Adjustable-Rate Mortgages (ARMs)

The adjustable-rate mortgage is a loan whose interest rate and payment are adjusted periodically over the life of the loan.

The initial interest rate of the ARM is lower than that of a fixed-rate loan. The borrower usually can choose from a variety of adjustment intervals, ranging from six months to five or seven years. The shorter the adjustment intervals, the lower the initial rate on the loan will be.

ARM rates are based on an "index," which is a published market rate such as the U.S. Treasury bill or the Prime Rate Index. Because ARMs are indexed, it is designed to fluctuate with changing economic conditions and changes in the index used by the lender. This means that a low ARM today might go higher or lower as the rate is adjusted according to the terms of your mortgage contract. The index reflects the current cost of lending money and is easy to find out at any given time because it is published in your local newspaper. The lender also adds a margin, which represents its profit on the loan, to the index to establish the loan's fully indexed rate. At the time of the agreed-upon adjustment interval, payments may go up or down according to the fully indexed rate.

ARMs are not all alike. That is why it is particularly important for you to take the time necessary to evaluate what you want and need in a home loan and compare the various ARM programs available. Because the terms and requirements of ARMs vary so dramatically, you should ask the lender to review with you the various features and conditions, including the down-payment amount, the duration of the loan, the maximum loan amount, and whether gifts can be applied to any costs associated with the loan.

Although the ARM may be well suited for a wide variety of home buyers, there are a number of circumstances under which it may be a particularly wise option. For instance, the ARM may be a good choice for a prospective buyer who anticipates an increase in his future income. In that case the ARM's low initial interest rate enables the buyer to qualify for a higher loan—and thus get more house for his money—and his risk is relatively low because his future increased income will be sufficient to cover a rise in interest rates and monthly payments. Because ARMs provide for a lower initial interest rate than other mortgage loans, it may also be recommended for those individuals who plan to remain in their home only a short period of time. Finally, for the home buyer who believes that interest rates will remain the same or go lower in the years ahead, the ARM may be an excellent financing choice.

ARMs are particularly attractive during periods of high interest rates because they allow a borrower to purchase a home at lower than the current interest rate. Perhaps the greatest advantage of an ARM is that it provides flexibility to help meet a borrower's individual needs. The ARM often enables a buyer to qualify for a larger loan because lenders may make the decision based on current income and the first year's payments, which may be low because of the initial interest rate.

Although riskier than a fixed-rate mortgage, an ARM ultimately may be less expensive over the long term if interest rates remain steady or move lower. Because the interest rate applicable to an ARM moves up and down with market conditions, there is no need to refinance if the interest rates decline.

The risk, and potential drawback, of the ARM, of course, is that an increase in interest rates would lead to higher monthly payments in the future. That is why it is extremely important to determine the *maximum* amount that your monthly payment could increase under the terms of your ARM. Your loan agreement will include a cap, which is a limit on how much your interest rate or monthly payment can change, either at each adjustment or over the life of your loan. This cap provides protection from drastic rate fluctuations. If by using the interest rate cap, you determine that the highest monthly payment you may have exceeds your ability to pay, then the ARM may not be the best choice for you.

It is also important to determine the consequences of early repayment of your loan. Some ARMs carry a penalty for early repayment. This might be a significant drawback for home buyers who would like the option of paying back their loan early.

You should ask your lender to review the various conversion options with you as well. Some ARMs have a conversion feature that allows the borrower to convert the loan from an adjustable to a fixed rate within a certain time frame. Be sure to inquire about any fees charged for converting the loan.

Finally, in the event you want to sell your house to another home buyer sometime in the future, you should find out if your ARM is assumable. A loan is assumable if you are allowed to transfer the mortgage to the new purchaser. Although most ARMs are assumable, it is nevertheless important to determine if yours is assumable by a qualifying buyer at the same terms as your loan.

Jumbo Loans

Some lenders offer jumbo loan programs for borrowers seeking loan amounts typically over $200,000. Because this exceeds the maximum allowed by conventional loan guidelines, lenders offer jumbo loan programs to individuals who meet certain income, down-payment, debt-ratio, and credit-history criteria. Jumbo loans are available using fixed- or adjustable-rate options. Check with your lender for the specific details of its jumbo loan program.

Balloon Mortgages

Balloon mortgages offer a low fixed rate for the first five or seven years of the loan. At the end of this term, you may pay off the loan in a single lump sum or balloon payment, or refinance the loan. Some balloon-loan agreements allow you, for a modest fee, to convert the loan to a fixed rate. The new fixed-interest rate then remains in effect for the remaining years of the loan until it is paid off.

One advantage of this type of loan is that it offers a lower interest rate than fixed-rate mortgages, enabling the borrower to qualify for a higher loan amount. Additionally, for at least the first five or seven years of the loan, the borrower is able to count on stable monthly payments.

The balloon mortgage may be an especially good choice for a borrower who is interested in short-term financing at a low rate or who wants to pay off a mortgage loan quickly.

The potential drawbacks concern the costs involved in refinancing or converting the loan at the end of the five or seven years. The borrower faces the risk that interest rates may be high at the time the loan must be refinanced.

VA/FHA Loans

VA and FHA loans are mortgages that are insured by the Veterans Administration and Federal Housing Administration, respectively. These government agencies work with lenders throughout the country, making it possible for many first-time home buyers and buyers on modest incomes to finance homes.

VA and FHA loans offer both fixed and adjustable rates, as well as varying term lengths, depending on the program. FHA loans require up-front insurance premiums and a small down payment. VA loans are available to qualified military veterans, certain military personnel, and widows or widowers of veterans. They require no down payments and are available to eligible purchasers more than once.

Because of the flexible qualifying guidelines, it is easier to qualify for VA and FHA loans than for a conventional fixed-rate loan. Both VA and FHA loans have lower closing costs than other mortgage loans. Additionally, like other fixed-rate mortgages, fixed-rate VA and FHA loans can ensure stable and predictable monthly payments because the interest rate is constant over the life of the loan. Some FHA loans are assumable if sold to qualified buyers.

FHA loans have several special requirements. First, you, as the borrower, must intend to live in the home being financed by the FHA loan. Second, your mortgage amount cannot exceed FHA's maximum mortgage amount for the area where you are buying the home. Finally, you are subject to debt limits, which means that your total monthly debt payments, including your mortgage, can equal up to 41 percent of your monthly pre-tax income. Your mortgage payment alone can be up to 29 percent of your income.

The minimum down payment required for an FHA loan ranges from 3 to 10 percent, depending on the program. The maximum loan amount varies by locale and is typically lower than the amount available with other types of loans.

VA loans have two special requirements. Loan amounts may not exceed the limit set by the Veterans Administration, which is currently $184,000. Like FHA loans, your monthly debt payments, including your mortgage, cannot exceed 41 percent of your monthly pre-tax income.

Reverse Mortgages

The reverse annuity mortgage—or reverse mortgage, as it is commonly called—is available to and uniquely suited to older people, especially retirees living on fixed incomes. This type of mortgage enables older homeowners to convert the equity in their home into monthly payments that are paid back only when the borrower or the borrower's spouse (whoever remains longer) dies or moves from the home.

Reverse mortgages allow an older homeowner to draw on the equity of their home in either a lump sum, regular monthly payments, or as needed from a line of credit without making payments on the mortgage. A reverse mortgage provides disbursements to the homeowner until a pre-established principal limit (based on the value of the equity in the home and the owner and spouse's anticipated term of occupancy) is reached. After the principal limit is reached, the mortgage stops making payments and simply continues to accrue interest on the outstanding principal and interest until the home is vacated by the owner or spouse. (Reverse mortgages typically allow homeowners and their spouses to remain in the home until death or until they decide to move from the home.) When the home is vacated by the homeowner or his/her spouse, the mortgage and accumulated interest must be repaid, usually by the sale of the home or by a relative who buys or inherits the home. Reverse mortgages are available at either fixed or variable interest rates and may be conventionally insured by a lender or insured by the Federal Housing Administration.

The way the program works is as follows. Your home is appraised by a lender to determine the amount of equity you have in the home. The lender then consults actuarial tables using your and your spouse's ages to determine the approximate period of time that you and/or your spouse is likely to continue residence in the home. Based on these calculations, the lender sets a maximum loan amount calculated to insure a buffer between the total mortgage amount, including interest accrued during the mortgage term, and the anticipated value of the home's equity when the owner and or spouse vacate it.

You may use the money you receive from the lender for any purpose, including covering household expenses or paying for health care. The advantage of this type of loan is that you receive lump-sum, monthly, or on-demand tax-free payments. The disadvantage of the loan is that the principal limit may be reached before you die or move from the home. This could leave you without a cash stream that you have come to rely on. A further disadvantage for someone who needs only a small mortgage amount or a mortgage for a short period is that the fixed up-front mortgage initiation costs (appraisal, title search, etc.) are very expensive when amortized over a short period or small mortgage amount.

Moderate-Income Programs

Many lenders offer programs designed to help first-time home buyers or those with low to moderate incomes finance a home. Generally, it is easier to meet the qualification and down-payment requirements for these programs. Discussed below are a number of the most common programs. Because the qualification requirements and terms of these loans and programs vary from one location to the next, you should check with your lender to find out about the programs in your area and whether you may be eligible for a loan under one of these programs.

The Community Home Buyer's Program

The Community Home Buyer's Program (CHBP) is a government-backed program administered by the Federal National Mortgage Association (often called FNMA or Fannie Mae). Lenders across the country, in cooperation with Fannie Mae, offer loans to potential buyers meeting certain requirements. The qualifying guidelines are flexible, allowing buyers to purchase a home with less income and lower closing costs than are required for other types of mortgage loans. Additionally, the program allows borrowers who have not established a traditional credit history to demonstrate good credit practices through timely payments to landlords and utility companies.

The CHBP allows you to borrow up to 95 percent of the appraised value of a house or the sales price, whichever is lower. The maximum loan amount for most states is $203,150, although lenders may elect to offer a maximum amount that is lower than the state's maximum. You may obtain a 15- or 30-year fixed-rate mortgage. Although loans offered under the CHBP are conventional fixed-rate loans, they differ from standard conventional loans because you are not required to have two months of mortgage payments in reserve after closing. This means you need less cash at settlement.

You are responsible for making a down payment of 5 percent of your loan amount. You have two options for coming up with this down payment. You may use your own personal funds exclusively, or you may use a combination of 3 percent of your own funds with 2 percent of funds from another source (often called a 3/2 arrangement). If you use the second option, different requirements may apply to you, so be sure to check with your lender. The permissible sources for the 2 percent include a gift or loan from a relative or a grant or unsecured loan from a nonprofit organization, public entity, or your employer.

There are several eligibility requirements that are common to all Community Home Buyer's Program participants. First, your total combined gross income cannot exceed 115 percent of the median household income for your area. Median gross income means that half the households earn more than you and half earn less. If your down payment consists of the 3/2 arrangement described above, your household median income cannot be more than 100 percent of the median household income in your area. Second, you must be purchasing a single-family home (this includes town houses, units in approved condominiums in planned-unit developments, and, under some programs, houses that you plan to rehabilitate for your own use) that you plan to make your principal residence. You may not own any other real estate at the time of settlement. However, you may sell your current home prior to settlement to satisfy this last requirement. Also, most programs require mortgage insurance.

Depending on which lender you use, there may be other requirements as well. Lenders have varying rules relating to closing costs. Some lenders allow closing costs to be paid for through a gift or grant from your family, a nonprofit organization, a government agency, or your employer. Other lenders may allow the seller to contribute up to 3 percent of the buyer's closing costs as well. In some situations, the lender itself may offer a program to finance 2 percent of the down-payment or closing costs, while other lenders prohibit the buyer from financing any portion of the closing costs.

Many lenders have a mandatory educational requirement for buyers seeking a mortgage through the CHBP. This requirement is usually satisfied through the buyer's attendance at a seminar or class on home ownership and personal finances. Borrowers who meet certain criteria do not have to attend an educational program. Those excused from the class include borrowers who have previously owned a home, borrowers who make a 5 percent down payment from their own funds, and borrowers who have savings after closing that are at least equal to two monthly mortgage payments.

CHBP loans share many of the advantages of a conventional fixed-rate mortgage. These loans ensure stable monthly payments and protection against rising interest rates. If you are a first-time home buyer with limited personal funds for a down payment and closing costs, you might want to contact your local lenders to see if you are eligible for this type of loan.

FannieNeighbors with the CHBP

The FannieNeighbors program is available to buyers who are purchasing a home within certain designated central cities or other specified eligible areas. This program was created by Fannie Mae to increase home ownership and promote revitalization in major cities and in minority and low- to moderate-income areas. Through this program you can obtain a mortgage loan at a lower rate and reduced fees when you buy in a targeted neighborhood. The Office of Management and Budget has published a list of central cities that you can obtain through your lender.

Like other CHBP programs, you need less income to qualify for a FannieNeighbors mortgage and less cash for closing. In fact, to qualify for loans in some cities, there are no income requirements.

Most of the eligibility requirements for the FannieNeighbors program are the same as the straight CHBP loans. The home must be your principal residence, and you must not own any other real estate. Additionally, borrowers must complete a home-ownership and personal-finance class sponsored by the lender. The maximum loan amounts are also the same under this program.

Hud Homes

The U.S. Department of Housing and Urban Development (HUD), a federal government agency, offers a program called the HUD 221(d)(2) program. The program offers fixed-rate loans with different term lengths available. Unlike the CHBP, there is no income limitation. You must intend, however, to make the home your primary residence.

HUD homes are available only to families. The government has defined a family as two or more people related by blood, marriage, or operation of law. For purposes of eligibility, persons over sixty-two years of age, handicapped, or forced by government action to move from their home are also considered a "family."

To qualify for a HUD home, you must be able to make a down payment of 3 percent of the purchase price, including closing costs. If you lost your previous home because of government action (e.g., the government needed to build a road through your property), no down payment is required.

The allowable debt limits are the same for a HUD home as for an FHA loan. That is, your total monthly debt payments, including your mortgage, can equal up to 41 percent of your monthly pre-tax income. Your mortgage payment alone can be up to 29 percent of your income.

In addition to the benefits associated with fixed-rate loans, including the comfort of predictable monthly payments and the avoidance of potentially dramatic interest-rate fluctuations, there are several additional advantages to purchasing a HUD home. HUD pays the real estate broker commission (up to 6 percent of sales price) and may pay many of your closing costs. HUD homes are priced at their fair-market value and are usually ready to move into. Moreover, HUD loans require no mortgage-insurance premium. However, a monthly premium is included in your mortgage payment.

HUD homes may be single-family homes, condominiums, or town homes. They come in a variety of shapes and sizes and are located in many different neighborhoods throughout your area. HUD works with lenders to create incentives to move into these homes. Some lenders offer as much as a $300 moving allowance. Others may even offer a rebate of up to 5 percent of the sales price (not to exceed a certain amount) for homes on the market for less than $40,000. Check your local newspaper for advertisements for HUD homes. The ads include many of the features of the home and may list attractive incentives.

CHAPTER 7

Evaluating Mortgage Lengths

Kathy and Bobby are middle-aged parents with kids in high school. They're thinking about buying a second home on the lake that they may someday retire to. The question is whether they should take out a thirty-year loan they might not be able to pay off during their lifetimes.

Linda is a young urban professional who's making real good money right now. As the years progress, she'll undoubtedly make lots more. While she may be able to afford it right now, she doesn't want to be strapped with an incredibly high monthly mortgage payment in case she meets someone and decides to have a family.

The preceding chapter familiarized you with different types of mortgages that may be available. As you continue your quest for the mortgage best suited to you, you'll next need to determine whether to obtain a thirty-year mortgage or a shorter-term loan, such as a fifteen-year mortgage.

Thirty-Year Mortgages Versus Shorter-Term Mortgages

There are trade-offs between long-term and shorter mortgages, and there are advantages and disadvantages to both types of mortgage products.

- The longer a mortgage lasts, the lower the payments will be.

- However, the longer the mortgage lasts, the more interest you will pay over the term of the mortgage on each dollar you borrow.

- Also, generally longer mortgage loan terms carry slightly higher interest rates than the shorter-term products.

- Further, the longer the mortgage lasts, the less each payment you make will reduce principal.

The following illustration graphically demonstrates this point. (Note: This illustration, and all others in this chapter, includes only the principal and interest portions of a loan payment. Hence, the following costs are *not* included in the calculations that follow: payments of insurance and taxes into an escrow account, payments of PMI [private mortgage insurance], which is generally required if a borrower borrows more than 80 percent of the value of the house.)

$100,000 Loan

	30-Year Loan, 8¼% Rate	15-Year Loan 8% Rate
Monthly Payment	$751	$956
Amount of Loan Still Owed After:		
1 year	$99,316.80	$96,402.20
3 years	$97,752.10	$88,285.80
5 years	$95,880.10	$78,766.30
15 years	$79,330.50	$0

Essentially, the shorter-term mortgage accomplishes two very worthwhile goals:

- *Considerably less interest is paid on the shorter-term loan.* This means that a much larger percentage of each payment goes to pay off the principal of the loan. Conversely, however, it means that you will have a smaller portion of each payment that you can use as a tax deduction.

- *A considerably larger portion of each payment is going back into your pocket as an investment in your house.* Because you are spending less on interest, for every dollar you are spending paying off your mortgage, you are leveraging that dollar and paying off your house loan quicker.

For example, assume you paid the $100,000 loan for fifteen years. After fifteen years on the 30-year note, (using the 8¼ percent rate illustrated in the above example) you will have paid:

- A total of $135,228.60 in payments

- $114,559.10 in interest

- Only $20,669.50 off on the principal of your note, leaving $79,330.50 still due

On the other hand, on the 15-year note, (using the 8 percent rate illustrated above for the 15-year note) you will have:

- Paid a total of $172,017 in payments

- Paid $72,017 in interest

- Paid the entire balance of the $100,000 note

The two significant drawbacks to a fifteen-year loan are:

- It has a significantly higher monthly payment.

- The value of the tax deductions available to help homeowners pay their mortgages is reduced because less of each dollar spent on the home loan is interest, so less of each mortgage payment is deductible.

You also may not want to pay off a house too quickly for a number of reasons. First, the value of the quicker loan payoff is only as good as the interest rate on the mortgage loan. In other words, if you have an 8 percent mortgage loan, you are only saving yourself interest on your money at the 8 percent rate by paying your mortgage back early. Careful investment strategies can often yield higher returns on money than your mortgage-interest rate. This, of course, assumes that you invest the difference between the lower thirty-year mortgage payment and the higher fifteen-year payment.

Second, the equity in a home is not readily accessible (unless you take out a home equity loan, which means that you are in effect paying someone else interest to use your own money). Given this, you might find many other more valuable uses for your money other than investing it in your home.

The underlying value of paying off your home loan early should not be minimized, however. This is a decision you should make as part of an overall savings plan. It is not a decision that is necessarily made at the same time you are obtaining a mortgage on your home. To avoid having to make this decision at the same time as you are deciding on your mortgage product, while still allowing yourself the opportunity to pay off your mortgage early at some future time, make sure your mortgage contract does not penalize you for prepaying the loan.

So long as there is no prepayment-penalty clause in your mortgage contract—and most federally insured mortgages do *not* include a prepayment penalty—you can obtain the longer-term loan and have the option at any time of adding to your payments. In this way you may enjoy the lower payments when your income and expenses require you to pay less on your mortgage. You can always ask and find out from your lender the required payment amount necessary to pay off your mortgage by a specified date. Then, if you so choose, you can make the larger payments to meet a targeted payoff date. If there is no prepayment penalty in your mortgage contract, you will always have the freedom to pay either the lower thirty-year rate payment or any higher payment that you choose.

Pay the Fifteen-Year Mortgage Back Early

If you are even considering a fifteen-year loan, that must mean that you are interested in the benefits of saving thousands on interest expense and paying your loan off early. If your loan does not have a prepayment penalty, you can always make *extra* payments to principal each month. You would be astonished at how much benefit the little bit of extra money you apply to your mortgage will provide for you.

For example, assume you are considering a fifteen-year loan, but decide against it because you want the added flexibility of the thirty-year loan's lower payments. Or, you may not qualify for the shorter-term loan because of the higher payments required. Under these circumstances you could voluntarily embark on a self-saving program in which you apply an extra amount each month toward your mortgage. The amount of your monthly mortgage payment could then rise each year by this extra amount. (Of course, at any time you could always reduce the monthly payment back down to the minimum payment required under the loan contract if you so choose.)

For example, on the $100,000 loan we have been looking at, let us say you increase your monthly payments after the first year by $25. After the second full year, you increase the monthly payments by an additional $25, so that you are paying $50 more than the minimum. In the fourth year, you increase your monthly payments by an additional $25, now paying $75 more than the minimum. Let us say you continue this yearly increase until your voluntary payments equal approximately what they would have been had you obtained a fifteen-year mortgage in the first place. Believe it or not, you would pay off your thirty-year loan after making these payments for only eighteen years and nine months.

Your voluntary payment schedule would then look like this:

$100,000 Mortgage
30-year Loan, 8% Rate
Minimum Payment $734

Monthly Payment Number	Year of Mortgage	Payment Amount	When Mortgage Will Be Paid Off
1–12	1	$734	360 payments
13–24	2	776	320
25–36	3	801	293
37–48	4	826	273
49–60	5	851	258
61–72	6	876	246
73–84	7	901	238
85–96	8	926	231
97–225	9–18	951	225

(Note: the monthly payment for a fifteen-year mortgage at the same interest rate would have been $956.)

The idea here is to increase your monthly payments at an incremental rate. In this way you will not really notice the effect of the added expense to your pocketbook, while still enjoying the flexibility that a thirty-year mortgage gives you in case of financial hard times. Some homeowners increase their mortgage payments based on a small proportion of their annual salary adjustment for inflation. Assuming your family has a $50,000 gross income, one year's 5 percent increase will yield an additional $208.33 gross income per month. The extra $25 toward the mortgage then seems a relatively painless method of achieving a loan-free home in less than nineteen years.

You can determine the amount of the additional payment that you need to make by increasing the original loan payment by .025% in the first and each additional year. So, for example, if your loan amount was for $175,000 at 8 percent for 30 years, your minimum monthly mortgage payment will be $1,284.50. The amount you need to increase the monthly payments after the first year, and each year thereafter, is $43.75

in order to pay your loan off in eighteen years and nine months.

The formula for this, so you can use it on any mortgage amount, is as follows: Figure .025% of the loan amount. This will be the extra amount you need to increase your mortgage payments by each year for eight years in order to pay the loan off in less than nineteen years. For example: .025% of $175,000 is $43.75. After the first full year's payment, increase the monthly mortgage amount by $43.75. After the second full year's payment, increase the amount by an additional $43.75. Keep increasing the amount each year until you have completed year 8. That year's increase of $43.75 will be the last increase. From the beginning of year 8 through the 225th payment (which should be 18 years and 9 months after you got the mortgage), your payments will be $7 \times \$43.75 = \$306.25$.

There is obviously no need to follow this regimen exactly. *Any* additional amount added to your principal each month will mean that you pay off your loan earlier than you would otherwise. A financial counselor, your loan broker, or most anyone with a spreadsheet software package on their computer can help you determine the effect of the extra monthly payments you wish to make. What's more, additional lump-sum payments specially earmarked to go against the principal amount owed will ultimately reduce the cost of your mortgage. So, if you inherit some money, get a hefty income-tax refund, or win the lottery, you might consider using some or all of the proceeds toward retiring some of your mortgage debt earlier than planned in your mortgage contract.

Addressing Basic Questions

Now that you know the pros and cons of a thirty-year mortgage versus a shorter-term one, how should you decide which option is best suited for you? Ask yourself the following question:

How does your current family income situation compare with what you reasonably expect your future income to be?

Find the answer that best suits your prediction:

1. *The current family income is at the lowest you reasonably expect it to be until retirement.* In this case, the lowest monthly payment mortgage makes the most sense. Assuming there is no prepayment penalty in your loan, you can always increase the amount of monthly payments you make in the future to pay off your loan early if you decide to do so.
2. *You are anticipating a reduction in income (or an increase in expenses) in the next few years.* In this case also, the lowest monthly payment mortgage is the best alternative. You need the maximum flexibility to meet the demands that anticipated reduced income will place upon your family budget.
3. *You expect your family income to remain about the same as it is currently, increased for inflation, until retirement.* In this case you might consider a shorter-term mortgage, because of the savings advantages inherent in these products. But this decision should be made as part of an overall savings strategy.

CHAPTER 8

Paying Points

Nell and Taylor discovered that they could get a mortgage at a lower interest rate only if they were willing to take a couple of "points." They wondered whether they should pay the extra points up-front or keep the higher interest rate for the life of the loan.

Deborah is confronted with a dilemma. She can only get the loan at the best available interest rate if she is willing to pay several additional points. The lender says he's doing her a favor by being willing to lend to someone with her credit and employment history.

Points and *discount points* and *prepaid finance charges* are all different terms that mean the same thing—fees paid by the homeowner to the lender at the time the mortgage is made. They represent a different kind of income to the lender from what you think of as interest—which is the money *earned* by the lender during the course of the loan for the outstanding debt. But points, discount points, and prepaid finance charges all represent income to the lender in exchange for making the loan. The same thing is true for mortgage brokers, for whom points represent a primary source of compensation. If points are reduced, the broker's or lender's profit margin is also reduced.

One point equals 1 percent of the loan amount. Two points equal 2 percent of the amount borrowed; three points equal 3 percent, and so on. For example:

1 point on a $100,000 loan   = $1,000
2½ points on a $100,000 loan = $2,500

Never assume that you cannot bargain with a lender or broker. You can always ask that points be reduced (as well as other fees and the overall interest rate on the loan). Lenders and mortgage brokers have considerably more discretion than you might think.

Basic Rules on Points

Here are some things to keep in mind as you consider the impact of points on your mortgage loan:

1. Since points are an additional method of compensating the lender for making the loan, all other fees paid to the lender, other than those paid out to third parties (such as for an appraisal, survey, or credit report) when the loan is made should also be considered "points" for the purposes of this discussion. For example, a fee called an "application fee" paid to the lender is considered by federal law to have the identical characteristics as "points." You should include all such fees in your calculations used to determine which lender to use and which loan product to obtain.

2. The number of points charged should be in direct relation to the interest rate charged on the loan; the higher the points, the lower the interest rate should be.

3. If you are purchasing the house and the seller is paying points, that does not necessarily save you any money. If you decide after you have completed the analysis recommended by this chapter that you would prefer *not* to pay any points, you should be able to convince the seller to reduce the purchase price of the house by the amount of money that the seller would have paid in points on your loan.

4. Whether you pay the points in cash at or before closing, or you finance the points (increase the amount that you borrow by the amount of the points), the points still cost you money. Indeed, as will be illustrated below, financing the points means that they are actually costing you more than their face amount—because in addition to paying back the points, you are also paying interest on the loan of money for those points.

Too Many Points Should Make Alarm Bells Ring

It is rarely, if ever, justifiable for there to be more than two or three points on a loan. If you are presented a loan with more than three points, you should carefully determine exactly what you are getting in return. Is it a lower interest rate? Are you getting a loan you would not be able to get from another lender without paying so many points?

A borrower's poor credit rating should *not* be used as an excuse by a lender to increase the number of points, as well as the interest rate, on a loan. Presumably the purpose of the points is to compensate the lender for the up-front costs of making a loan. In other words, the administrative expenses incurred by the lender in taking the loan application, overseeing the approval process, ensuring that the security (your house) is worth the necessary amount, and actually providing you the money that you are borrowing. *It does not cost a lender any more money to go through these processes if you have poor credit than it does if you have good credit.* The administrative expenses borne by the lender are the same. If a lender attempts to charge you an excessive number of points and uses your poor credit as an excuse, you should carefully shop with a number of different lenders to ensure that you are obtaining the best product available. (It should be noted that the same cautions regarding an excessive number of points also apply to loans with high interest rates. Poor credit is not a valid excuse for the charging of an excessive interest rate on your home loan.)

Remember, you are providing the best security available on any loan made—you are putting your house on the line. You are promising to repay this loan, and if you do not, the lender can take your house and sell it to pay the remaining amount due on your loan.

How Many Points Should You Pay?

For the majority of loans sold on the secondary market, which includes most federally insured loans, the rule of thumb is that on a thirty-year loan, each half point paid should reduce the interest rate on the loan by one-eighth of a percent. This results in the following differences in points, interest rates, and monthly payments for a thirty-year loan of $100,000:

$100,000 Loan for 30 Years
Points Versus Payments

Interest Rate	Number of Points	Cost of Points	Monthly Payment
8%	0	$0	$734
7¾	1	1,000	716
7½	2	2,000	699

In order for you to determine whether it is best to pay the points and achieve the lower interest rate or not pay the points and pay the higher interest rate on the loan, you must first make an assumption on which you can base your decision.

For how long do you believe you will keep this loan? A number of factors come into play here, including:

- How long will you remain in this house?

- Do you envision refinancing in the future to access more equity in your house or to pay for home improvements?

- Are current interest rates sufficiently low to ensure that you will not want to refinance in the next few years to lower your monthly payments?

You must assess these and related questions and come up with an operable assumed period in which you will keep this loan. That period enables you to determine the financial viability of paying points.

For example, assume that you decide that it is unlikely that you will refinance your home in the next five years. Also, you are fairly comfortable assuming that you will not be selling the home in the next five years. Five years then becomes the period for you to use to calculate the value of paying points.

Using the loan rates of 7½ percent with 2 points, and 8 percent with 0 points, illustrated above, we can see that *if you are comfortable with assuming you will keep the loan for five years*, paying two points may make sense. This is because the difference between the payments charged for these two loan products, totaled over the five-year period, exceeds the cost of the points paid:

$100,000 30-Year Loan
Costs of 2 Points After 5 Years

Loan Rate	Cost of Points	Monthly Payment	Total of Payments After 5 Years	Total Cost
7½%	$2,000	$699	$41,940	$43,940
8	0	734	44,040	44,040

This, however, is a close call. There is only a $100 difference between the total amount spent during the entire five years. This does not, however, take into consideration the time value of money (where the value of money is corrected to take inflation into account). That said, it can be assumed the value of $100 now exceeds the value of $100 five years from now. So in this example, it is probably not wise for you to pay points.

The scenario changes, however, if the length of time for keeping the loan is extended. In spite of the best of intentions, you may not be able to reasonably assume you will keep the loan ten years or more. It is possible you will want to refinance at a future date to take advantage of lower interest rates. Compare the above two loan products over a ten-year period:

$100,000 30-Year Loan
Cost of 2 Points After 10 Years

Loan Rate	Cost of Points	Monthly Payment	Total of Payments After 10 Years	Total Cost
7½%	$2,000	$699	$83,880	$85,880
8	0	734	88,080	88,080

In this ten-year comparison, it does indeed look like it would be worthwhile to pay the points up front and gain the advantage of the lower payment. If you decide to do this, however, you should remember that you will not see the benefit of the money you invested in points until *five* years later.

Bear in mind that the average mortgage loan is paid off in about seven years—either because the house is sold or the loan is refinanced. If you use the seven years as a yardstick, you find that it is of doubtful benefit to invest in the points:

$100,000 30-Year Loan
Cost of 2 Points After 7 Years

Loan Rate	Cost of Points	Monthly Payment	Total of Payments After 7 Years	Total Cost
7½%	$2,000	$699	$58,716	$60,716
8	0	734	61,656	61,656

Although the difference in the total costs expended over seven years between these loan products is almost $1,000

($940), the value of the investment in points is still dubious. This is so because of two factors. First, no one knows the future, and with every good intention and perfect planning, your evaluation of the chances that you will not sell your house or refinance this loan within seven years is subject to fate. If you are wrong, and you do refinance before the reduced payments have benefited you, you will have wasted the money you spent on points.

Second, the time value of money means that $1 today will be worth something less than $1 tomorrow. The factors involved in determining the time value of money are always subject to the question—what is the proper amount of inflation to factor in? Without engaging in this debate, one can see the questionable value of investing thousands of dollars today to buy down the monthly payments on a loan that you do not know how long you will keep.

Should You Finance Your Points?

Probably not. If based on the above discussion, you decided to pay points, you should be aware that the analysis is very different if you finance them. The actual benefit to you of the payment of points to the lender is significantly changed. In effect, the payment of the points is simply postponed until you sell the house or refinance this loan. In the meantime you are paying interest on the money you borrowed to pay the points. So the actual cost to you of the points is the *amount of the points, plus the interest on those points.*

All of the above illustrations assume that you have paid points on the loan in cash. If you add the additional cost of the points to the monthly payments, the equations change. The difference in the monthly payments for the loan in which the points are financed must be calculated.

$100,000 30-Year Loan
Cost of Points When Financed

Loan Rate	Points	Amount Financed	Monthly Payment	Total of Payments 5 Years	Total of Payments 10 Years
7½%	$2,000	$102,000	$713	$42,779	$85,560
8	0	100,000	734	44,040	88,080

At first glance this chart makes it look like paying the points, *and financing* them, may be the ticket. But look at the cost to you over time.

$100,000 30-Year Loan
Loan Amount After 5 years When Points Financed

Loan Rate	Points	Amount Financed	Monthly Payment	Total of Payments 5 Years	Amount Still Owed	Total Cost
7½%	$2,000	$102,000	$713	$42,779	$97,717	$140,496
8	0	100,000	734	44,040	95,880	139,920

Remember, the payment totals on the comparative loans when the points were *not* financed were only $100 apart. When the same amount of points are financed in otherwise identical loans, the result is that it is over $500 *more* expensive to buy down this loan with financed points than it would be to pay a higher interest rate with no points.

The equation changes only slightly when the loan is evaluated over a 10-year term:

$100,000 30-Year Loan
Loan Amount After 10 Years When Points Financed

Loan Rate	Points	Amount Financed	Monthly Payment	Total of Payments 10 Years	Amount Still Owed	Total Cost
7½%	$2,000	$102,000	$713	$85,560	$91,218	$176,778
8	0	100,000	734	88,080	89,430	177,510

So, for the cost of approximately one payment—$732—after ten years the value of the points, when financed, might turn out to benefit the borrower. But remember, you must factor into this calculation the certainty with which you can assure yourself that the loan will not be paid off through refinancing or sale of the house prior to the ten years. Also, the time value of money makes the payment of points in this scenario even less valuable to the homeowner than the bare-boned story of the numbers in these tables illustrate.

How Long Does It Take for Points to Pay Back Their Cost?

The examples used throughout this chapter show the proportional values of paying points. The lessons from these examples do not change if we change either the amount of the loans or the number of points involved. The significant numbers are only:

- The ratio between the number of points and the reduced interest rate purchased by the points

- The number of years the loan will be held

- Whether the points are paid for in cash or are financed

To illustrate: buying fewer points—say, only one point—would yield the same result. This is a very small payback after paying on the loan for five years. As the table below illustrates, the return is $80 after five years on the $1,000 investment in one point (assuming the point isn't financed).

$100,000 30-Year Loan
Costs of 1 Point After 5 Years

Loan Rate	Cost of Points	Monthly Payment	Total of Payments After 5 Years	Total Cost
7¾%	$1,000	$716	$42,960	$43,960
8	0	734	44,040	44,040

Assuming a half point buys one-eighth of 1 percent in the interest rate, the basic rules of thumb on the payback on points are as follows:

- It will take 58 payments (4 years and 10 months of payments) to pay yourself back the cost of the points *if the points are not financed.*

- If you finance the points, it will take 96 payments—eight full years of payments—to see the return from incurring the cost of paying, and financing, the points.

- These rules apply whether you are talking about one-half of one point or 3 points, and regardless of whether your loan is for $50,000 or $250,000.

Addressing Basic Questions

1. How long do you reasonably believe you and your family will be in this house?

Five years or less. If you believe that this is reasonably likely, there is no reason whatsoever for you to pay points. You should try to avoid paying as much closing costs as possible, including points. In some areas of the country, no closing cost loans are available in exchange for a slightly higher interest rate. These types of products would be most advantageous for someone in your position. You have only five years, or less, in which to amortize all the closing costs you incur, and it is doubtful that higher interest rates will cost you as much over this short period of time as the unamortized closing costs.

Approximately seven to ten years.   This is a slightly closer call, but it is still probably wiser for you not to pay points to buy down your loan. Given the marginal savings you will incur from the payment of points, along with reduced value of those savings because of inflation, the payment of points is unlikely to be of great financial benefit. Certainly, if you can pay the points in cash it is better than financing them. For some homeowners, however, there is considerable psychological value in having a lower monthly payment. If this is important to you, the financial returns on the payment of points certainly justifies the potential costs involved.

Twenty or more years. If you are this certain that you will stay in the house, the only remaining issue is whether it is possible that you will refinance the house in the next few years. Refinancing could be in the cards for any one of several reasons:

- You want to obtain a lower interest rate.

- You want to take out some of the accumulated equity in the house.

- You want to make some home improvements, and refinancing the first mortgage is the most financially sound way.

If any of these possibilities is likely to occur, then your analysis should be the same as if you expected to sell the house within this shorter period of time.

If, however, you are reasonably certain that you will neither sell the house nor refinance it for ten years or more, then it may make sound financial sense to buy down your interest rate by paying points. Again, you should carefully run the numbers and satisfy yourself that the reduced monthly payments will justify the higher up-front costs involved in the payment of points.

2. How does your current family income situation compare with what you reasonably expect your future income to be?

The current family income is at the lowest you reasonably expect it to be until retirement.   If this is the case, it would not be wise to incur the extra expense for the payment of points. Paying the extra cash at closing will only squeeze you more, and it will take at least five years of reduced payments to see the benefit of those points. Moreover, financing the points at closing will have even less benefit. It will take almost five and a half years for the dollars invested in the points to yield a net return in savings in payments. And that net return does not factor in the time value of money, or the risk you run of possibly selling or refinancing prior to that time.

You are anticipating a reduction in income (or an increase in expenses) in the next few years.   The strict financial analysis does not really change depending upon your personal situation. The value of a dollar to you may change, especially psychologically. If you are expecting your income to be reduced in the upcoming years, it may be worth your investment now to save on future monthly payments. You have the money, and you may not have it then. Consider this: what would you do with the money that you would otherwise spend on points now? If you would invest it, and then have that investment, as well as the earnings on it, it would be best to *not* spend it on points. But if you would spend it on something else, yet there is emotional value to you in knowing that your monthly payments will be lower in the future when you will have the reduced income, it may be a very prudent investment to spend the money on points, and lower your interest rate and monthly payment for the future.

You expect your family income to remain about the same as it is currently, increased for inflation, until retirement.   In this case, there is really very little impetus for you to buy the points. It makes little financial sense and does not present a good return on your investment in the points.

CHAPTER 9

Mortgage Lock-ins

Charlene was recently preapproved for a mortgage in the amount of $175,000 by her lender. Since the rate of the loan was "locked-in" at the mortgage-interest rate in effect on the date her preapproval was granted, Charlene shouldn't have to worry about future interest rate increases if she closes on her new home within sixty days.

Carol and Gary recently found the home of their dreams. Indeed, to make the home even more attractive to prospective buyers, the owner had gotten a mortgage lender to "lock-in" a very attractive interest rate.

"Locking-in" an interest rate is one of the most important aspects of the home-buying process. This is especially important in circumstances when interest rates increase between the time when the mortgage is applied for and closing occurs. By securing a lock-in, a prospective homeowner obtains an interest-rate commitment from the lender that the rate in effect at the time the contractual relationship was entered into remains in effect for a set period of time, usually fifteen, twenty, thirty, forty-five, or sixty days.

As the above examples illustrate, there are different types of lock-ins with which you should become familiar. These include the following:

Traditional Floating Rates

Suppose you have found a house that you really want to buy. After selecting a mortgage lender and submitting your mortgage application, your rate and points "float" up or down during the weeks or months prior to closing in response to changing economic conditions. For example, if mortgage-interest rates rise, the interest rate you will ultimately be charged with increases as well. Similarly, if mortgage interest rates decline, so will the rate charged on your home loan. With such a floating approach, you are at the mercy of changing circumstances that may or may not increase the ultimate cost of your loan. If mortgage-interest rates have been fluctuating up and down, you may luck out with circumstances in your favor when you go to closing. Accepting a floating rate is probably your best bet if mortgage rates are headed downward at the time you file your application. Instead of committing yourself to the higher rate in effect when you apply, you may be able to get a considerably lower rate if you lock-in immediately prior to closing on your new home. Conversely, interest rates may start heading back up again prior to closing. So, there are no guarantees. While this approach obviously adds some uncertainty, it can save you a lot of money.

While floating rates may still be available, they may no longer be necessary. Rather than needlessly exposing yourself to possible interest-rate spikes, you might consider pursuing the different types of lock-ins discussed below. There may be no need to delay your pricing decision during the weeks or months it may take you to locate a home and sign a sales contract on it.

Traditional Rate Locks

Imagine yourself in the same circumstances as above—you have found a house and a lender. Instead of accepting a floater arrangement with the lender, you lock-in the loan rate and points in effect at the time you submit your mortgage application. Instead of the interest rate fluctuating, the pricing components are "locked-in," or guaranteed, for a set period of time prior to closing. Locking-in is particularly important if interest rates have been steadily edging upward at the time you begin discussions with a lender. In such circumstances it's probably likely that mortgage-interest rates will continue to increase in the future.

Traveling Rate Locks

Before finding a house you wish to purchase, you may still be able to lock-in a loan rate and terms while you shop around or while you're negotiating a deal with a seller. Some traveling rate locks protect you even before you've found a piece of property or before you've even applied for the loan. As you search for your new home, your locked-in rate travels with you. Such an approach insulates you against interest-rate increases while you're out surveying the housing market. Indeed, if interest rates go up while you're shopping, you have a loan guarantee (at a lower interest rate than you could find when you ultimately purchase) available to you. When you find your house, you've got a loan guarantee in your pocket.

Many traveling rate locks expire after a certain number of days. For example, your rate and pricing terms may be guaranteed for thirty days. During this time you can go out, shop for a home, and negotiate a sale price. Then, if you've located a property during this initial thirty day period, you may also be able to extend the lock-in for an additional forty-five to sixty days depending upon the type of mortgage you are applying for.

Variations on this theme exist. Some lenders may lock-in prospective homeowner pricing for a period of seventy-five to ninety days. At any point during this period the buyer can lock-in at a current rate for a set period (e.g., sixty days).

During this sixty-day period, if interest rates decline, the buyer's rate can float downward. But if interest rates increase, the rate can never go higher than the locked commitment rate.

House Rate Locks

Some mortgage lenders approve mortgage rate locks that are attached to certain pieces of property. For example, a homeowner may negotiate a mortgage deal with a lender at the time the home is put up for sale. Under this arrangement, the home's sale comes with its own mortgage terms attached. As a result, the seller may advertise that the home comes with "rate protection" attached. This action can shield potential home buyers from interest-rate increases. If the buyer qualifies within thirty, forty-five, sixty, or ninety days (depending upon the particular lender's requirements), he or she will receive the interest rate locked-in at the time the lender and homeowner negotiated the mortgage contract. Since the rate ultimately received will probably be lower than the rate currently available, the house becomes a more attractive purchase option.

If you can find a rate-protected home that you like, you can either accept the terms negotiated by the seller and the mortgage lender or go out and find your own mortgage financing. If you accept the terms attached to the sale of the house, you should be on the lookout for any additional costs (i.e., higher points) that may be associated with the locked-in rate.

Lock-in Length

In general, the longer the lock-in time period, the higher the points charged at a given rate. For example, you might be able to lock-in an interest rate for a period of as long as sixty or ninety days. The rate on this longer lock-in loan, however, may be higher (e.g., a half point higher) than a fifteen- to twenty-day lock-in at the same rate. Lenders traditionally charge extra for longer lock-ins because of the greater risks they assume if rates increase during the covered period.

With mortgage lenders hungry for home-buyer business, more and more of these innovative lock-in programs can be expected. The key is to find something that meets your needs and time frame. You obviously need to be on the lookout for the increased costs that are associated with many of these creative new programs. You may wind up paying anywhere from a quarter of a point to a couple of points for the privilege of locking-in. You will need to make the necessary calculations to determine the type of lock-in most advantageous to you.

Be a lock-in conscious consumer. As you shop around for different pieces of property or for mortgages, ask about the different types of lock-in programs available. Real estate agents, mortgage bankers, mortgage brokers, and home sellers may be able to identify different types of lock-ins available that you might consider.

Lock-in Delays

Justin had gotten a lock-in on a home loan from a particular lender. Since interest rates had increased considerably, he was particularly excited about the incredibly low rate he had negotiated. But a couple of days before he was scheduled to close, his mortgage lender started requesting all sorts of information about the property he was purchasing and his financial status. Because of this, his closing was delayed and he was relegated to a mortgage at a much higher interest rate.

If interest rates increase significantly after a prospective home buyer has already locked-in a lower interest rate, there is very little incentive for a lender to hurry into writing a loan at a rate that is considerably less than prevailing rates. In such cases, buyers with locked-in rates may find themselves subjected to

delays that result in the failure to close the loan during the prescribed locked-in period.

From the lender's perspective, it just makes good business
sense to collect all of the necessary information in order to
qualify the loan, even if it takes longer than expected. If
interest rates jump after a lock-in agreement has been signed,
lenders find it in their interest to scrutinize such loan applications more carefully. Problems on the application or with the
property that might have been ignored assume increased significance. From the borrower's perspective, delays may appear
deliberate since they have the practical effect of pushing settlement dates beyond the expiration of rate locks. In circumstances of rate-lock lapses, the lender is not obliged to honor
the lower rate originally agreed upon and no longer available.
Instead, the lender may propose a loan on completely different, higher, current-market terms.

If your lender requires you to meet certain loan-documentation
requirements, you should not be suspicious. The fact that this
information is being requested does not necessarily mean that
your lender wants to back out of its loan commitments to you.
Most lenders require a variety of information before a loan can
be processed and often have legitimate reasons for requesting
additional information to support your application. Since these
requests may require you to hunt and dig for information, you
may feel that you are being unnecessarily burdened and inun-
dated with heavy documentation requests. This may not be the
lender's fault. The lender must make certain that the approved
loan can be sold in the secondary market. To do this, documentation of certain information may be required to make the loan as
strong as possible.

This may never happen to you. If you've gotten a lock-in on a
mortgage, however, it's probably in your best interest to protect
yourself nonetheless. The following actions are suggested:

Stay on Top of Your Mortgage Application

Once the lines of communication have been opened
between you and the person at your mortgage lender's who will

be processing your loan, keep these lines of communication open. There shouldn't be long gaps in time when you aren't talking with each other. Stay in close contact through regular telephone conversations, letters, and faxes with the person who is processing your loan. Document important conversations by sending a timely follow-up letter to the loan officer summarizing recent transactions and whatever information the lender has given you verbally. You might state in your letter, "It is my understanding that XYZ Mortgage Company has _____." Then fill in the blanks accordingly depending on the issue or issues under discussion. Specifically ask that they notify you in writing if they do not agree with any of the statements you have made in your correspondence. Creating such a paper trail makes it far more difficult for lenders to come forward suddenly with complaints about matters that have already been resolved.

Be on the Lookout for Common Delaying Tactics

There are several common delaying tactics used by lenders with which you should be familiar. These include:

Appraisal challenges. A common lender ploy is to question the appraisal, which serves as the basis for the value of the property being financed. Since different appraisal methods can be used, the lender may question the assumptions contained in the first appraisal and may even demand that the property be re-appraised or that the appraisal be reviewed. For example, appraisals are often based on comparable properties in the same neighborhood. The lender may challenge whether the comparable properties used were the correct benchmarks for assessing the value of the property to be purchased. Property appraisals are not instantaneous; they can take days or even weeks. This eats days away from precious loan-processing time. New appraisals can either confirm the property's worth or result in a devaluation of the property. In such circumstances, the lender may only be willing to loan a smaller amount of money. Since this may significantly increase the required down payment, the buyer may be left with no choice but to back out of the deal or to accept drastically different terms than originally envisioned.

Excessive documentation. Some mortgage lenders may require that every *t* be crossed and every *i* dotted on an application before it will be approved. While relatively minor errors are often ignored by lenders, rates that are rising far beyond those locked-in may be cause for lenders to balk at approving less than perfect loans. Because of this, borrowers sometimes find themselves having to hastily submit employment-verification letters, copies of bank statements, and required signatures at the eleventh hour.

One way you can protect yourself is to make certain that all of your documentation is in pristine condition when it is submitted. After the loan officer has had an opportunity to review materials submitted, press him or her to identify areas where additional information may be required. You should then provide this information as quickly as possible. Remember, you are responsible for making certain that small discrepancies and omissions do not result in a delay of closing beyond the lock-in date. Your best defense is often a strong offense.

Incomplete Income and Debt Information

All prospective homeowners may find themselves subjected to requests for additional income and debt information. Income information may be far easier to come by if you are employed and your employer can attest to your salary. Self-employed borrowers, people with income that's hard to substantiate, and applicants with complex financial situations may find themselves having to scramble to find such information. Credit-report entries may need to be explained or additional information provided. Federal and state income tax returns for a number of years may be requested. Partnership agreements, signed contracts, accountant statements, and other documents may need to be submitted before a loan will be approved.

In anticipation of having to provide these kinds of information, you should probably pro-actively assemble any pertinent information so you have it at your fingertips should it be requested by the lender. Any information you have access to that either verifies your income or indicates that a debt has been paid or the manner in which it was repaid may be useful.

CHAPTER 10

Applying for a Mortgage

After Robert had shopped around and found the best mortgage available, he was confronted with a mountain of blank forms. Not only was he required to fill out these forms, but he was also expected to supply personal information about various aspects of his life going back several years. In addition, he needed to provide evidence corroborating the information he was to provide.

Hopefully, you used the steps outlined in the preceding chapter to find the correct mortgage and lender for you. After you do this, the next step will probably be to sit down and meet with your loan officer. This is the lender's representative who will see you through the mortgage-application process. The loan officer's job is to collect information that the lender will need to process and hopefully approve your loan.

The loan application will be the loan officer's primary focus of attention. You may have been provided a copy of a loan application to fill out before coming to this meeting. If so, the loan officer will probably review your responses in the initial interview. Or the loan officer will go through the loan application, either filling it out for you or assisting you in completing the information requested.

Don't be intimidated by the mortgage loan application form. These normally request confidential data about your current and past employment, credit experience, past mortgage and former landlord experience, and any savings and investments you hold. You will be asked to provide information about yourself as well as your spouse and/or any other co-borrowers.

To avoid potential hassles and delays in getting your application approved, you need to make sure that the information on your application is as accurate and complete as possible. If you're like most people, you may not be able to recall off the top of your head the original loan amount and account number for a loan on a sofa that was purchased five years ago. You are probably not able to recite your credit card numbers, to give lender addresses for many of your current or past credit obligations, or to recall precisely your payroll history since you first began to work. Because of this, it's in your best interest to do your homework to make the mortgage-application process move along as smoothly as possible. So, come to the initial interview prepared. Going through old receipts, finding past pay stubs, and bringing along copies of your most recent income tax filings will probably serve you well in the long run. The mortgage loan application process can be completed much more easily and accurately if you take the time to prepare for the initial interview ahead of time.

In spite of your best efforts to dig up all of the information that you think might be needed, you will probably overlook something that the lender will ask for. Because of the variety of the different types of information needed by a lender to process your application, don't get your hopes up that one search will yield all of the information that the lender may ultimately require. You should be prepared to dig through additional files in search of missing items. If you can't locate information to the satisfaction of the lender, you may have to ask past creditors and others to supply you with the information required.

If you fill out the application yourself, you must make an effective presentation. To assure that the creditor can read the information you provide, it is probably best to type your responses on the credit application. If this is not possible, print legibly. Give all the information requested. If you do not know some of the answers, such as the number of a former account, go through your files or call your former creditor to get the information. If you are having trouble responding to questions in the spaces provided on the application, add an attachment. Be sure to place a notation in the appropriate space on the application so the creditor will refer to the attachment for that item. Do not skip any items. Because an incomplete application may yield a rejection, be sure to provide all the information requested so your application can be evaluated on its merits.

Before meeting with your loan officer, you will probably want to review the following section, which identifies the types of information you'll want to assemble for this interview. If you make a good-faith attempt to assemble the identified information and take it with you to the interview, you should be prepared to respond to most of the questions that will be asked of you.

Purchase Contract

Your loan representative will need you to provide important information that fully describes the property you are purchasing and the parties to the transaction. As a result, you need to provide your lender with the information described below. All of these items should be reflected in your purchase contract. If they are not, consult the seller or the realtor. The information you'll need to provide includes the following:

1. Any addendums, signed by all parties, showing the full names of the sellers and buyers as they will appear on the new deed, the amount of the purchase deposit, and who is responsible for closing costs, origination fees, etc.
2. If the house is not yet built or is under construction, you will need to provide a set of plans and specifications.
3. You will need to provide information identifying the precise location (i.e., street address, lot and plot number), age, and full legal description of the property.
4. You also will need to give your lender the name, address,

and telephone number of the real estate agent you've been dealing with and/or the seller of the property.

Your lender needs the above information to have an appraisal made of the property you plan to purchase. An appraisal is necessary to determine the value of the property that will serve as security for your loan.

Personal Information

Your loan officer will want basic information that will help the lender to confirm your identity and to get an idea of where you've lived and how you've handled your accommodations expenses in the past. You will need to provide the following information:

1. Social Security numbers of you, your spouse, and any other co-borrowers.
2. Proof of your age (bring along your birth certificate).
3. Educational background (copies of diplomas, degrees, professional accreditations may be needed to corroborate).
4. Your marital status.
5. Number and ages of your dependents.
6. Your current address and telephone number.
7. Name, address, and telephone number of your current landlord or mortgage lender.
8. Current housing expenses, including rent, mortgage, utility, real estate tax, and property payments.
9. Your former addresses and telephone numbers dating back seven years, if you have lived at your current address less than two years.
10. Names, addresses, and telephone numbers of former landlords or mortgage lenders over the past two years.

Employment History and Sources of Income

Your prospective lender will want to look at all of your sources of income. Indeed, one of the lender's primary responsibilities is making certain that you have the income to manage your proposed new mortgage payments should your loan application be approved. In addition to making sure you can afford the mortgage payments, lenders also want to be certain that you'll be able to afford the additional costs associated with home ownership (e.g., taxes, upkeep, repairs). Income information required includes:

1. At least two years' employment history with employer's name and address, your job title or position, length of time on the job, salary, bonuses, commissions, and average overtime pay.
2. Recent paycheck stubs and federal W-2 forms for two years.
3. Proof of outside income, including compensation from part-time work, income from business ventures, rental income, Social Security or disability payments, child support, etc. (cancelled checks, copies of recent checks, copies of leases or deeds, certification of benefits, divorce decrees, or similar evidence may be required for each source of income).
4. Records of dividends and interest received from investments.
5. If you are self-employed, full tax returns and financial statements for two years. A profit and loss statement for the current year to date as well as copies of signed contracts that generate income may also be required.
6. A written explanation if there are gaps in your employment record for various reasons (e.g., illness, disability, loss of job, seasonal work).
7. Copies of your federal and/or state tax returns for the past two years may also be required by some lenders.

If you fill out the loan application yourself, list your gross income (before any deductions), unless you are specifically requested to indicate the amount of your take-home pay (net income). Make sure your income is stated in the increment requested (annual, monthly, or weekly). If you receive pension or government benefits, list the amounts you receive.

In addition to providing this information, you will probably also be requested to sign a Verification of Employment (VOE) form. A copy of this form will be sent to your current employer for completion. If you've been at your current job for less than two years, a copy of this form will also be sent to your previous employer. You will also be asked to sign a general authorization that gives your lender authority to check into your employment background and to obtain other information concerning your reputability.

Personal Assets

The next thing you need to provide is verification of all of your assets. To this end, provide a detailed listing of all assets that you either hold individually or with someone else. Thus, if you and your spouse own a house together or have a joint savings account, list them on the application. Do not include the original value of these assets. Rather, estimate their current value, since they may well have increased since you acquired them. If the house you paid $50,000 for has a current market value of $125,000, list the latter figure. Indicate the estimated current balance in your savings or investment accounts, inclusive of interest and other earnings. The following information should be provided:

1. All insured banking accounts (checking, savings, money market, certificates of deposit) you own, along with the name, address, and telephone number of the institution where they are held, the names on the accounts, account

numbers, current balances, and account statements for at least the last two statement periods.

2. All uninsured products (mutual funds, stocks, bonds, annuities) you own, along with the name, address, and telephone number of the location where these investments are held, the names on the accounts, account numbers, current balances or market value, and account statements for at least the last two statement periods.

3. All retirement accounts (individual retirement accounts, Keoghs, simplified employer pension plans, 401(k), employee stock ownership plans, vested retirement and pension plans) you own or held for your benefit, along with name, address, and telephone number of the location where these investments are held, the names on the accounts, account numbers, current balances or market value, and account statements for at least the last two statement periods.

4. Face amount and cash value of life insurance policies.

5. Make, model, year, and value of all vehicles in your possession (including original purchase price, amount currently owed, and name, address, and telephone number of title or lien holder).

6. Address and market value of all real estate owned, along with the amount of rents collected, the outstanding mortgage on the property, the monthly mortgage payments (profit and loss statements will be required for all investment properties).

7. Value of other personal property (e.g., home furnishings, jewelry, computer equipment).

In addition to providing this information, you will probably also be asked to sign a Verification of Deposit (VOD) form for each of the insured and uninsured accounts you have listed above. These forms will be sent to the institutions you have listed to confirm the existence of your account and its current balance. Instead of being asked to sign separate VOD forms for each account you hold, you may also be asked to sign a general authorization that gives your lender authority to make inquiries of any institutions holding your deposits.

Personal Indebtedness

You should make certain to provide a listing of obligations on which you owe money. These will include:

1. All of your credit obligations (e.g., secured and unsecured personal loans, credit cards, lines of credit on bank accounts, automobile loans, department store charge cards and loans, gasoline credit cards, and any other obligations on which you owe an outstanding balance) from banks, savings and loans, finance companies, retailers, credit unions, and other creditors, including the name, address, and telephone number of the creditor, the account or loan number, outstanding balance, maximum allowable balance (on open-end credit), monthly payment, and the number of payments remaining.

2. All of your mortgage-related debts (e.g., mortgages, second mortgages, and home-equity loans), including the name, address, and telephone number of the lender, the account or loan number, outstanding balance, maximum allowable balance (on open-end credit), monthly payment, and the number of payments remaining.

3. All obligations for which you may ultimately be held responsible (e.g., co-signer of a note, joint credit obligations).

4. All obligations that require you to make payments to others (e.g., child support, spousal maintenance, alimony).

5. All court proceedings involving the collection of a debt you owed, or any foreclosure or bankruptcy proceedings, actions, or judgments in which you have been involved within the past seven years, including the name of the court, action taken, amount and date of the judgment,

copies of pertinent court orders, filings, other documents, etc.

You will want to make certain that your lender has as complete a picture of you as possible when determining the fate of your application. To this end, make certain to verify any information that may be difficult for your lender to obtain. For example, if you are now married, remarried, or have changed your name, you should provide your lender with information about your former name and any credit history you may have had under that name.

Bear in mind that you cannot selectively list your favorable accounts and fail to mention any unfavorable obligations you may have. Since credit reports from several different credit-reporting agencies will be requested by your lender when your application is reviewed, it's a pretty sure bet that your lender will find out about all of your prior accounts. So it's not in your best interest to try to hide any unfavorable entries. To put as positive a spin as possible on your application, you might list your best credit accounts first on the application, making certain to include both individual and joint accounts. If you were an authorized user on an account, list the account along with your authorized-user status.

Provide the current balances due for each of your obligations rather than the original amount of credit extended. Thus, if you took out a $15,000 car loan three years ago and have one year left on the loan, indicate today's balance rather than the original amount.

If you have unfavorable credit accounts (those you did not pay in a timely fashion, which appear as adverse entries on your credit report), you must identify them. However, if you feel that these do not accurately reflect your creditworthiness, explain this to your potential creditor. For example, suppose you got behind on your bills during a period of unemployment. Now you have a stable job and make twice what you made in your old position. If your creditor knows this, the negative accounts can be viewed in light of the extenuating circumstances. Most lenders recognize that unemployment, death, illness, incapacity in the family, divorce, separation, and other difficulties may temporarily impair your ability to make timely payments on your outstanding credit obligations and will take such circumstances into consideration when determining the fate of your application.

If the problem has been corrected and your payments have been made on time for a year or more, your credit will probably be judged satisfactory. Chronic late payments, judgments or loan defaults, and overextension of credit obligations, however, severely damage your credit rating, and may result in future credit applications being declined.

Keep Copies of All Information You Submit

You will probably need to refer to information provided should you need to follow up with the lender or pursue an appeal. Also, since your application will be likely to include valuable information about your credit condition (account numbers, balances, and so on), keep a copy of it for general reference. Then, whenever you need this information (e.g., if you apply for another loan or refinance your home at some point in the future), you will have the information at your fingertips and won't have to go hunting for it all over again.

Also, provide the creditor with any additional information that might enhance your chances for approval. For example, if your credit history is scant, bring evidence of favorable credit experiences, like former accounts, accounts under former names, accounts at previous addresses, or paid bills. Or substantiate assets by bringing in recent bank statements, a copy of the deed to your house, a copy of your most recent tax return, evidence of income from different sources, or similar documentation.

CHAPTER 11

After You Submit Your Application

Julia filled out and submitted her mortgage loan application several weeks ago. Her prospective lender has contacted her a couple of times and requested additional information to process her loan. Although she has given the lender everything that has been requested, the wait is excruciating. Every time the phone rings, she expects the worst. What is taking so long?

Mortgage loans are significant long-term obligations. Depending on the size of the loan and individual lender practices, your lender will either hold the mortgage or sell it to the secondary mortgage market. Whether the mortgage is held by the bank or sold, the lender is responsible for the accuracy of the loan documents. To protect themselves from future liability, mortgage lenders are very careful to make certain that all information on your loan application checks out and that there is no missing information.

The lender's responsibility is to collect information that indicates whether you are likely to remain true to your repayment commitments (making your monthly mortgage payments in a timely fashion and eventually paying off your loan as prescribed under your mortgage loan agreement). As a result, a lender may request additional information or take more time to approve your loan application than you think necessary.

Once a creditor has your credit application in hand, it is "scored" to determine if you will be a good credit risk and

whether you will be extended credit. Your prospective lender
has three primary goals:

- To verify the information provided on your loan application

- To review credit information on you from independent
sources

- To determine the value of the property you are purchasing, since it will serve as collateral for the loan

The Loan-Approval Process

Everything in the mortgage-lending industry is in a state of
flux. Three factors are responsible for this climate of change.
First, the present mortgage processing system is outdated. It is
very labor-intensive, and even when computerized, it is slow
due to the need for outside verification of income, employment status, value of the property, etc.

Second, the mortgage industry is increasingly affected by the
trend toward bank mergers and acquisitions. As more and
more lenders become part of large corporate structures, there
will be constant pressure to streamline and increase the volume
of loans processed. These pressures will mean new procedures,
new staff, and inevitable confusion.

Third, technology may reduce the number of parties involved in mortgage transactions. For instance, it is possible
that mortgage brokers will be eliminated, replaced by your
realtor, who will give you a computerized list of all available
mortgage lenders and their current rates. Your lender may
have her own in-house appraiser (many already do) and not
even charge for the service—since most of the necessary information is already available from the city or county assessor's
office on-line.

With fewer and larger lenders processing more mortgages,
efficiency may rise through volume and use of state-of-the-art

technology. Competition for consumers may combine with technological efficiencies to reduce processing fees and speed up processing. All this will eventually be good for the consumer. It may be quite confusing in the next several years, however, as the industry changes and lenders respond with their own solutions and at their own pace. All this is to tell you that the following description of mortgage processing is how the industry works in 1996.

The Application

During application, the loan originator takes the information you provide at face value. If you say you make $50,000 a year and have $10,000 in the bank and that you have a contract on a house worth $125,000, the loan originator makes a determination on your eligibility based on what you say.

Conditional Commitment

Upon submission of your application and review of your credit report, your lender's underwriter (decision maker) will generally give a conditional commitment. This means that if you really make $50,000, if you really have $10,000 in the bank, if your house is really worth $125,000, and if your ultimate credit report and any necessary letters of explanation are sufficient, then you will get your loan. While underwriters look at your credit report before the conditional commitment, they take a more detailed look at your credit history during the processing. Be sure to request a conditional commitment so that you do not stay with a lender to completion if you are really heading toward denial of the loan.

Processing

From conditional commitment, your application goes to a processor. You will be assigned a person who will make sure that every piece of information that is necessary to close your loan is in place. It is at this stage that you will be expected to prove that you have a job or business, show that the income you said you have is really on your W-2's, or on your income tax Form 1040 if you have your own business. Your employer will have to complete a form that you really work for the company, your bank will have to verify that you have the money in the bank, and so forth.

Appraisal

At the same time your house will be assigned to an appraiser. The purpose of an appraisal is to establish the value of the property. This is because the property serves as collateral to secure the loan. If you are paying for the appraisal, you may have the option of picking an appraiser from a list of approved appraisers. If so, you can negotiate timing and cost. Occasionally, lenders have their own appraisers and do not charge extra for the appraisal.

Underwriting

When all verifications are in and an appraisal completed, the loan then goes back to the underwriter for final review and approval.

Required Mortgage Insurance

If you are approved, but are borrowing 80 percent or more of the value of the property, the lender will generally require you to have mortgage insurance. The lender requires this insurance because the cushion between the loan amount and the resale value has been reduced, exposing the loan to more non-repayment risk should you default.

In conventional 80 percent loans, the buyer's 20 percent equity serves as a cushion should property values decline or the house sustain damage. This is the case because the bank's loan is repaid first, before the owner's equity, when the house is sold to settle a loan default. In loans with lower down payments, however, a smaller cushion exists, and a bank's likelihood of full repayment falls should a default occur. Therefore, lenders generally require borrowers to purchase mortgage insurance to protect their loan principal from potential losses.

FHA and VA come with public mortgage insurance, and a direct endorsement lender approves the public insurance concurrently with approval of the loan. If your lender is not a direct endorsement lender, your completed loan file will have to be sent to FHA or VA for approval.

If you are obtaining a conventional mortgage, you will need private mortgage insurance (PMI), and your loan file will be sent to a private mortgage insurer.

Understanding private mortgage insurance. You have to be approved for private mortgage insurance, and the requirements of insurers generally parallel the requirements of loan purchasers on the secondary market. There are many private mortgage insurers, and they all have printed standards. The number of available insurers generally depends on the population of the area in which you live.

The lender generally selects the insurer, even though you pay for the insurance. In this instance the lender generally has your interest at heart because PMI is needed for the loan the lender hopes to initiate. Insurer's requirements are taken into account before lenders issue a conditional commitment. Therefore, if there are no surprises during the processing, there should be no surprises regarding the availability of private mortgage insurance.

Optional Mortgage Insurance

If you are borrowing less than 80 percent of the home's value, the lender will likely suggest you buy mortgage insurance designed to pay off the mortgage should you die or become disabled. By law, you are not required to purchase this insurance. Credit-life and credit-disability insurance is often quite costly, and the likelihood of needing this insurance during the mortgage term may be fairly remote. What's more, you may already have disability insurance through your employer that will serve a similar purpose.

While purchasing life and disability insurance may be appropriate under some limited circumstances, insurance purchasing should be done in the context of comprehensive financial planning, not as part of a home-purchase decision. Before purchasing credit-life or credit-disability insurance, develop a long-term financial plan and then determine if these insurance products fit that plan. Should you decide to purchase credit-life or credit-disability insurance, make sure to shop for the best rates and terms.

Property Insurance

The lender generally requires hazard insurance on your property (insurance for fire, vandalism, or other destruction of the property) to protect the collateral (your home) that is securing the loan. The lender will require this policy to be in the amount of the mortgage principal, and the policy will name the lender as beneficiary. You are responsible for obtaining property insurance for the lender and will be required to provide evidence of coverage for your loan file. Shop around, since prices vary considerably.

You will also want to purchase property insurance to cover the difference between the mortgage principal amount and the total value of the home. This policy protects your investment in the property and will name you as the beneficiary.

Tips on Making the Process Work for You

Understanding Mortgage Processors—Why They're So Picky

You cannot come out of this experience without wondering if the processor gets paid based on the thickness of your file. They want proof of this and proof of that and everything in between. However, this is not the fault of the processor. Over 95 percent of all mortgages are sold to investors (the secondary market) and are not held by the lender originally making the loan.

Lenders typically make their money on loan initiation fees, not mortgage-interest payments. Freddie Mac and Fannie Mae (two federally chartered secondary-market mortgage purchasers) buy the majority of home loans. Insurance companies, Wall Street investment firms, and others buy the balance. Lenders like this arrangement because they can make a profit on the initiation, get their principal back, and use it again to generate more initiation fees. This allows banks with limited capital to expand profits through a high volume of initiation fees rather than simply collecting a set interest rate on a relatively static pool of capital.

Each buyer in the secondary market has a set of standards that the loans must meet, and these require extensive documentation. When the secondary market buys a batch of loans from a given lender, they spot-check a random sample of files. If any are not perfect (according to their standards), they can return all the loans. Obviously, lenders don't want all of last month's loans returned because they are already using the money from the sale of last month's loans for this month's loans. Thus, it is the job of the processor to make "perfect loan files," including all the forms for the documentation required by secondary-loan purchasers.

You will have a good relationship with your processor if you quickly and efficiently respond to each request for more information, even if you are sure that it is unnecessary, unwarranted, or think it borders on plain harassment. It's good if your processor is contacting you. If you don't hear from your processor, then you should worry. If you are frequently contacted, at least you know your loan processing is progressing. If not, call and see if they have received all the verification forms. Ask how your loan is coming. Do they need anything else?

The processor may also order a report from a special credit agency that services mortgage lenders. This agency looks at credit reports from at least two different sources and verifies the data on the reports. This agency also looks for any discrepancies that may indicate duplicity or other items "of concern" to the lender. If something that concerns the lender is found, you may be asked to respond. It is advisable to ask, frequently, how your in-depth credit check is coming along.

If there are any problems, discuss them with your loan originator and respond as soon as possible with a letter of explanation. Hopefully, any problems that arise can be explained as an unusual occurrence and something that is not likely to reoccur. Perhaps it is not even your fault—an error on the part of the creditor or on the part of the credit agency. Place top priority on finding and explaining any blemish on your record. An unresolved blemish on your credit can be fatal to a mortgage application (see Chapter 3).

Getting Involved in Your Appraisal

Like the processing, take a pro-active role in your appraisal. If you can, select your own appraiser. Talk to several before making your choice. Be sure you request a copy of your appraisal (you are entitled to it under Regulation B of the Equal Credit Opportunity Act). If nothing else, it is filled with interesting information. Generally, even if the appraiser thinks your house is worth far more than you are paying for it, the appraised value will be at the sale price in your contract. Only if the appraiser thinks your house is worth less than the sale price will the appraisal indicate a different value. If the appraiser values the home at less than the contract price, you may not be able to borrow as much as you had planned. For example, if you had planned to borrow $95,000 (95 percent of $100,000) and the value comes in at $96,000, you'd only be able to borrow $91,200 (95 percent of $96,000).

If your appraisal comes in below the price that you have agreed to pay for the house, you have three choices. First, you can appeal the appraisal. Obtain and go over the copy of the appraisal very carefully for possible errors. Talk to your loan originator's supervisor or head of lending in your area about any errors you find, and suggest a second appraisal.

Second, your contract to buy is generally contingent on your ability to get a mortgage based on a specific appraisal value. If the appraisal value is below the agreed-upon sale price, you may be able to renegotiate the sale price with the seller, or you may be able to nullify the contract without penalty.

Third, if the appraisal is lower than the selling price and the seller does not want to lower the price, you have the option of paying the difference between the appraised value and the sale price. In the example above, you can increase your down payment from $5,000 to $8,800, and the lender will loan you $91,200.

If Your Application Is Approved

If your loan is approved, you will receive a commitment letter from the lender. This letter is your formal loan offer. It will include:

- The loan amount (appraised value less your down payment)

- The term of the loan (number of years in months)

- Any loan-origination fees or points (bank fees based on a percentage of the loan amount)

- The annual percentage rate or APR (the real interest rate including fees and points)

- The monthly charges, itemized, including principal and interest, taxes, and insurance

Go over the commitment letter carefully. Make sure you understand it, that it is exactly as you expected, and that you will be able to comply with the conditions of the loan. By signing the commitment letter, you accept the terms and conditions of the loan offer.

You will then have two time commitments. First, you will have a set amount of time to accept the loan. Second, you will have a set amount of time to close the loan.

If you have any problems, talk them over with your loan officer before you sign. Remember that at any point in time before you sign the commitment, everything is still negotiable. You are the buyer. Make sure you are satisfied.

CHAPTER 12

Closing Costs

Zina is calculating how much money she will need to buy a house so she can decide if she can buy this year. One thing she is not certain about is how much money she will need to cover closing costs. Friends have mentioned lots of different charges (e.g., appraisal fee, inspection fee, title fees), but she is not sure how many there are and which she will have to pay.

When you find a home that you want to buy, you will make a purchase offer to the seller. Once the seller of the home accepts your offer in the form of signing it, the offer becomes the sales contract for the transfer of the home from the seller to you.

The agreement that you reach with the seller relates to the sale price of the home. The sales contract also covers many of the important details of the settlement of the home purchase. Settlement, or "closing," as it is often called, is the final step of the home-buying purchase and the point at which you take ownership of the property from the seller.

Settlements may be conducted by lending institutions, title companies, escrow companies, real estate brokers, or attorneys. In most cases the party that conducts the settlement represents the seller. You are entitled to have an attorney represent you at any or all stages of the sales transaction including settlement.

Depending on the area where you live, either the seller or the purchaser of the home will cover the closing costs associated with the sale of the home. The buyer and seller are free to negotiate the fees and decide who will pay what portion or all of the closing costs. Because there are many costs associated with settlement or closing, shifting the responsibility for payment of some or all of these fees can greatly impact the final cost to the buyer, as well as the total income from the sale for the seller.

Once the seller accepts your offer, you likely will begin searching for a mortgage company to finance your purchase (if you have not found one already). It is important that you become as informed as possible about the various types of mortgages available from the different mortgage lenders.

When shopping for a lender, inquire about the specific settlement services that each lender requires. Some lenders require title insurance or a new survey or charge you for a credit report or appraisal, while others do not. Additionally, some mortgage lenders recommend that you engage the services of title companies, appraisers, attorneys, or others whom they trust and with whom they regularly conduct business. Whether you are allowed to select your own provider of settlement services or whether the lender designates whom you will use, be sure to determine if the rates you are being charged are competitive in your area.

Also, remember that the real estate agent involved in your transaction represents the seller and not you, the buyer. Hence, the realtor's primary goal is to get a signed contract in hand. The real estate agent may recommend that you deal with a particular lender, title company, attorney, or other provider of settlement services. Do not just accept their suggestions but, rather, investigate the reasons why they recommend these particular individuals and do some shopping around on your own.

Once you find a lender that you want to work with, you will file a loan application. Within three business days after receiving your completed mortgage loan application, your lender must comply with the Real Estate Settlement Procedures Act of 1974 (RESPA), a federal law, by providing you with a good-faith estimate of all the possible fees and costs of settlement services.

Your lender must also give you a copy of the U.S. Department of Housing and Urban Development's guide on settlement costs at that same time.

The HUD guide contains a settlement statement that includes a financial worksheet which you may want to review thoroughly. By working through your purchase transaction on the worksheet, you will be able to calculate the total estimated cash you will need in order to complete the purchase of your new home.

It is important that you carefully review the estimate and ask your lender about any fees you do not understand. You should not wait until you are signing the necessary papers at closing to inquire for the first time about questionable fees.

Between the time you submit your loan application and you close on your new home, you will have an opportunity to shop for settlement services. Although the investment is not as large as actually purchasing a home, settlement costs add up, so it is important that you find a company that will give you the best deal for your money.

Keep in mind that some fees associated with settlement are unavoidable no matter how good a loan you get. For instance, fees for title searches, appraisals, credit checks, insurance, and flood insurance are standard for most loans. Nevertheless, you should still be aware of such costs and compare them with the fees that other lenders in your area charge. Even though they are legitimate fees, the margin that lenders add in order to make a profit may vary, which provides some flexibility in your ability to negotiate for lower fees.

Lender-Imposed Fees

There are also several mortgage-related closing costs associated with your loan. These are often imposed by your lender at the time you apply for your mortgage loan. First, you must pay an application fee that covers the initial costs of processing your loan request and checking your credit report. The second fee relates to the appraisal of the home that you are planning on buying. The lender will also require that an independent surveyor verify that your lot has not been encroached upon by any structures (for example, a fence crossing over the property line) since the last time a survey was conducted on the property.

You will also be required to pay a loan-origination fee for the lender's work in preparing your mortgage loan, as well as discount points at closing. Check with your lender to determine the number of points you will be charged.

If you make a down payment of less than 20 percent of your loan amount, you will likely also be required by your lender and perhaps in accordance with the laws of your state to take out mortgage insurance. This covers the lender's risk in the event you fail to pay your mortgage each month. Premiums may be paid in a lump sum at closing, annually, or are added on to the amount of your loan payment each month.

Finally, your lender will require by the time of closing that you have homeowner's hazard insurance. This will protect you against physical damage to the house by fire, wind, vandalism, and other causes. You may also have to cover an inspection fee for an evaluation of the structural condition of the property.

Title Services

Your lender will not give you a mortgage loan unless you can show that the seller of the home owns it. This is because your lender wants to be assured that you are purchasing the home from the actual owner and that there are no outstanding claims against the property you are buying. To prove that ownership exists free and clear of any claims, an escrow or title company or an attorney conducts a title search of the property.

Because public records relating to real estate are spread among several government offices, the title search covers county courts, tax assessors, surveyors, and recorders of deeds. Additionally, records of deaths, divorces, court judgments, liens, and will contests must also be reviewed, since all of these can affect ownership rights of the property in question. If you are one of the fortunate buyers who resides in an area where all of these records are integrated on a computer, then the title search may be completed relatively quickly.

In addition to the title search, you may also be required to purchase title insurance to protect the lender against any errors made in the title-search process. The cost of the one-time insurance premium is usually based on the loan amount and is usually paid by the buyer. Just as with other settlement-related costs, however, you may be able to negotiate and shift some or all of this cost to the seller.

If title insurance is required, you will also want to find out if the title insurer will either conduct, or arrange to have conducted, the title search for you. Because the title insurance required by the lender protects only the lender from undetected claims and other title problems, you may also want to consider purchasing your own title-insurance policy to protect you from such unforeseen difficulties. The cost of your premium likely will be only a fraction of the lender's policy; however, this usually varies from one locale to another.

As with other mortgage-related services, shop around for title services. When shopping for title insurance, you should take a close look at two important features. First, try to find the best rate for the policy itself. This will vary depending how much competition for title services there is in your particular area. Second, you should closely examine the coverage of the policy. Select the policy that has the fewest exclusions of situations where the insurer will not cover your title problems.

You can negotiate with the seller about who pays for title and other settlement service costs. Although there is no set formula for determining which party is responsible for which fees, there may be a certain customary way things are done in your area. If your sales contract does not address the various responsibilities of each party, operate on the assumption that they are open to negotiation. Of course, other factors figure in to the equation. For instance, if the seller is desperate to sell the house, you likely have additional leverage. If, however, the home has been on the market only a short time and is sought after by numerous buyers, the seller may have the upper hand in the negotiations.

Government-Imposed Fees

In some parts of the country, government-related fees can make up the bulk of your settlement costs. For instance, in some areas, transaction-recording fees, transfer taxes, and property taxes collected by local and state governments may be quite large. Obviously, you cannot legally avoid paying these costs, but you may be able to negotiate with your seller and shift a portion or all of these fees in his or her direction. It is important to remember that you should propose this and other fee shifting at the time you make your offer to purchase the property.

The sales contract itself contains many provisions that govern the sale and purchase of the home. Prior to signing the sales contract, it is vital that you make sure it correctly reflects your agreement with the seller. As the buyer, you are allowed to make changes and additions to the contract. For example, if your contract does not already contain one, you may want to add a clause in which the seller provides assurances that all of the heating, electrical, and plumbing systems and appliances are in working order, and that your future home is structurally sound. You will probably also want to consult with an attorney about the contract. That's because once it is signed, you are bound by its terms.

Although the total bill for settlement-related services may vary from loan to loan and from area to area, figure that at least an additional three percent of the sales price of the property will be added through settlement costs. In higher tax areas of the country, settlement expenses may increase the bill by five percent to seven percent. In any event, make sure to weigh the potential cost of settlement into your sales offer. Moreover, you should shop around for as many of the mortgage- and settlement-related services as possible. Finally, to the extent possible, negotiate as much as you can in order to shift some of the settlement costs to the seller.

CHAPTER 13

Refinancing, Home-Equity Loans, & Second Mortgages

Refinancing

Refinancing a mortgage, simply put, is paying off an existing mortgage and taking out a new one.

Why Refinance Your Mortgage?

You might consider refinancing your mortgage for several reasons:

Interest rates have fallen. Interest rates may have fallen since you got your mortgage, and you want to lock in a lower rate to save money and/or lower your monthly payment.

You need lower payments. Interest rates are comparable to when you got your mortgage, but you want to lower your mortgage payments by extending the term of your mortgage.

Conversion to a fixed rate. You may have an adjustable-rate mortgage and want to switch to a fixed rate for predictability.

Accelerated repayment. If you want to increase your monthly payment amount to pay off your mortgage more quickly, you may be able to obtain a lower interest rate by refinancing rather than simply making extra payments.

Need money. You may have accumulated equity in your home (through appreciation or mortgage repayment) that you want to take out of the home to use or invest elsewhere.

Money management. You may have high-interest, non-tax-deductible consumer loans (credit card balances, auto loans, student loans, home-repair loans, or even home-equity loans) that you want to pay off using lower-interest, longer-term, tax-deductible mortgage debt.

Refinancing your mortgage may allow you to accomplish these goals dependent on:

- Current interest rates
- Initiation costs (points, credit-check fees, title-search fees, attorney fees, appraisal fees, and transfer taxes) of the new mortgage
- Current level of equity in your home (home value less mortgage obligations)
- Length of time you have held your current mortgage
- How long you plan to remain in your current home

The following information and examples will help you understand what specific issues to examine when you are considering refinancing. To do your own calculations, use the mortgage table in Chapter 5 for payments and call your mortgage banker for initiation fees (the ones in the examples are merely illustrative; yours will vary substantially).

Refinancing Because Interest Rates Have Fallen

Justin has had a $100,000, thirty-year fixed-rate mortgage for five years now. Interest rates are much lower now (7 percent) than they were when he bought his house (9.25 percent). A bank is willing to refinance Justin's loan for thirty years at 7 percent, *charging 2 points. Justin makes a few calls and learns that his origination fees will be $500, credit-check fees will be $100, title-search fees will be $200, attorney fees will be $400, appraisal fees will be $300, and there will be no transfer fees. He plans to sell the house in five years and wonders if he would save money by refinancing in the interim.*

A fall in interest rates can mean large monthly and overall savings on your mortgage payments if you can lock in a lower rate. Depending on how long you intend to own the home, however, the cost of refinancing may be high enough to negate potential benefits. Let's examine Justin's situation and see if it makes sense for him to refinance. To do this, Justin must:

1. Calculate the cost of refinancing (amortized over the sixty months—five years—he intends to keep the home)
2. Compare the difference between his current payment and the total of the new payment plus the amortized costs of refinancing

Refinancing Costs

Points: 2 points on $95,880	$1,918
Loan Origination Fees	500
Credit Check Fees	100
Title Search Fee	200
Attorney's Fees	400
Appraisal Fees	300
Transfer Taxes	0
Total fees	3,418
Lost interest on 3,418 for 5 years @ 5%	968
Total Cost	4,386
Total fees amortized over 5 years	$73/mo

Cost Comparison

Current monthly payments: $100,000
@ 30 years @ 9.25% fixed interest $823

Effective refinanced monthly payments
$95,880 (remaining mortgage principal)
@ 30 years @ 7% fixed interest ($638)
plus amortized monthly costs of $73 $711

Cost Difference: $823 − $711 $112

Under these circumstances Justin would capture net savings of $112 a month by refinancing. If he was planning to own the home for only two additional years, however, the refinancing costs would rise to $183/month ($4,386/24) for a total monthly payment equal to $821 ($638 + $183). At an effective cost of $821, refinancing does not save Justin any money even though the comparison of the new and old payments might at first appear favorable. In fact, given the benefits of the mortgage-interest deduction (see Chapter 14), he may be better off with higher monthly payments if his initiation costs for the refinancing are not tax-deductible.

Refinancing to Lower Your Monthly Payment

Betsy and Bill are going to have a baby. Betsy wants to work part-time after the baby is born and thinks they should refinance their mortgage to lower their monthly expenses. They have had their current $150,000, thirty-year mortgage for fifteen years. Their interest rate is 8 percent and their payments are $1,100. Their principal balance is $115,000. Betsy has estimated that the total initiation cost will be approximately $4,000. She expects to roll these into the loan for a total principal amount of $119,000.

Refinancing may reduce your monthly mortgage payment depending on:

- The current interest rate
- Your principal balance
- The term of the new mortgage

If you extend your mortgage term (the surest way to reduce your payments), you will pay more in total interest before payoff. This is because you are extending the period of time for which you must pay the bank to use its money. For Betsy and Bill, refinancing could have the following results:

Term	Monthly Payments $119,000 Principal @				
	6%	7%	8%	9%	10%
20 years	$853	$923	$995	$1,071	$1,148
25 years	767	841	918	999	1,081
30 years	713	792	873	958	1,044

If Betsy can find a mortgage rate of 8 percent for her refinancing, her new payment for a thirty-year loan would be $873/month compared to her current payment of $1,100. If you are refinancing because you are about to reduce your income, refinance before you leave your job or cut back your hours. The better you look financially on your application, the more likely you are to get the loan.

Refinancing to Convert to a Fixed Rate

Constance has an adjustable-rate mortgage. In the ten years she has had it, she had paid anywhere from 5.5 percent interest to 9.5 percent. When her mortgage interest exceeds 7.5 percent, Constance has a hard time juggling costs and has to cut back on other expenses. If her rate went above 10 percent, she is not sure she could make her payments. Fixed rates are currently around 7 percent, and Constance has decided to lock in for her own peace of mind.

Many homeowners hold adjustable-rate mortgages. These have interest rates that typically adjust at regular intervals (e.g., semi-annually, annually, every two years) to the current prime rate (or sometimes to an English rate called LIBOR) plus a specified premium. Adjustable-rate mortgages usually have lower interest rates than fixed-rate mortgages. Homeowners can face severe increases in their monthly home payments, however, if interest rates rise substantially. Using the preceding chart, if rates on a thirty-year adjustable-rate mortgage of $119,000 jumped from 6 percent to 8 percent, the mortgage payment would increase 23 percent (from $713 to $873 a month).

To mitigate this risk, homeowners often chose to convert (i.e., refinance) their adjustable mortgages to fixed-rate mortgages when they can, especially during low interest-rate periods. This is a reasonable strategy if you operate on a limited budget and cannot afford a substantial increase in your mortgage costs.

Refinancing Instead of Accelerated Repayment

As an investment strategy, some homeowners decide to make more frequent payments or larger payments than their current mortgage requires. Supplemental payments are an excellent cost-saving and equity-accumulation strategy for homeowners who:

- Occasionally have extra cash available

- Cannot qualify for the higher payments that a shorter loan term would require

- Would prefer not to be committed to higher payments on a regular basis

If, however, you are making supplemental payments currently (or thinking about it) and you can qualify for higher monthly payments, you might want to consider refinancing for a shorter period (ten to fifteen years). Shorter-period loans typically have significantly lower interest rates. This will obviously commit you to a higher monthly payment throughout the loan period, but will save on interest payments two ways: through a lower interest rate and shorter loan period.

Refinancing Because You Need Money

The principal factor to remember in refinancing is that this is a mortgage on your house and often your largest single investment. Be wise (conservative), not foolish (taking risks). You don't want to lose your house by putting more debt on the house than you can afford.

As a rule of thumb, borrowing with your house as security should be limited to investments such as: major house repairs or improvements, putting yourself or a child through college, or operating your own business. To generate additional income, there is no cheaper way to borrow money than by refinancing. Second mortgages, installment loans, and credit card loans will all result in substantially higher monthly payments. By refinancing, however, you will make those payments for a very long time and substantially increase your interest payments over time.

Should you refinance or take out a second mortgage? A second mortgage for $50,000 would cost about 10 ½ percent interest (when the going rate in first mortgages is 8 percent). At that rate you will probably be required to pay it off in five to ten years. For a ten-year loan, monthly payments will be $675. The actual interest paid over ten years will be $31,000. Let's say, on the other hand, you've lived in your house for ten years. You had a thirty-year mortgage, your interest rate is currently 8 percent, your balance due is $100,000, and you have twenty years left to pay. You've paid off some of your original loan, and your house has also grown in value. Instead of taking a second, you refinance, taking a new mortgage for $150,000 at 8 percent for 20 years. You would get $50,000 cash, and your payments for the additional $50,000 will be $418 a month instead of $675.

On the down side, the actual interest paid for the $50,000 over the twenty years will be $50,320, but if you can only afford

$418 a month and you need $50,000—this is the best way to get it. That is why there are thirty-year mortgages—to bring the payment down to what people can afford. If you refinanced the $150,000 at 8 percent for 25 years, the additional monthly payment would be $322 a month; at 8 percent for 30 years it would be $265 a month.

Finally, if you take a second mortgage, you are usually limited to an 80 percent loan-to-value (LTV) ratio. This means that the first and second mortgages can equal only 80 percent of the value of your house. If you refinance, you can borrow up to 95 percent of the value of your house.

Short of your roof falling in, borrowing for home repair, college costs, or your own business can be planned in advance. Since mortgage rates vary considerably over the course of a year or two, you can carefully study the market and do comparative shopping. Then make your move when the market is at its best. You are looking to pay the lowest interest rate and the lowest closing costs (application, appraisal, title search, and points). Move when the rates are right, putting the money in savings and investments you can easily access while you are waiting to use it. One caveat: if you are refinancing in order to leave a well-paying job, be sure to refinance before you leave your job! That way your current income will serve as the basis for the loan.

Refinancing for Better Money Management

You should follow interest rates just as you probably follow CD rates or the stock market. If interest rates in the marketplace go above your interest rate, sit tight and enjoy your position. If rates go below your current interest rate, however, you should do everything possible to take advantage of the improved market. Most lenders will not contact you and suggest that you refinance. It is up to you to keep abreast of the market.

When, and at what rate, should you refinance? There is no rule of thumb because there are so many different circumstances. If, for example, you expect to live in the house for the foreseeable future, refinancing for only one point in interest rates makes good sense. If you have an 8 percent loan and the rates go down for a brief moment to 7 percent, grab it—just be sure you call around and get the lowest possible closing costs. If you have twenty-five years to go on a mortgage with a balance of $100,000 and you reduce your interest from 8 percent to 7 percent for twenty-five years, you will save $780 a year and $19,500 over the twenty-five years.

If you expect to live in the house for only a short time, look at both the cost of refinancing and at the prepayment-penalty provision of the new mortgage. If you have a prepayment penalty on your refinanced mortgage that extends for three years and you may sell in less than that time, you could lose your advantage for refinancing.

The same is true if you have an ARM. Since these loans are usually priced below market to begin with, they are most likely to go up before there is any chance that they will go down. Therefore, what might be a good deal for two or three years is unlikely to be a good deal for the life of your loan. Therefore, if you intend to be in your house for several years or more, carefully watch the market and move into a fixed-rate loan when you find one at a good rate.

The Mechanics of Refinancing

Shopping for refinancing is exactly the same as shopping for a mortgage. Plan to shop until you drop and, whatever you do, do not wait until you must refinance. Refinancing is something that can usually be planned. The more time you have for research, the better deal you will make.

In order to refinance, your credit must be good and you need income (preferably jobs) that justifies your monthly payments plus any debts. It is just like buying a house all over again, except that there are no special programs. You basically have to meet all of a particular lender's standards. As you know, these vary from lender to lender. After you have polled dozens of lenders, call your present lender back to see if he or she will meet or beat your best offer.

The more often you refinance, the more comfortable you become with the fact that a mortgage is just a commodity that you buy and pay off, as it suits you. On the street are all kinds of deals. When business is good for mortgage sellers closing costs go up (e.g., application, appraisal, and points). When business is slow for mortgage sellers, or they need cash, closing costs go down. At any given time you can usually find lenders who need to generate more business and are willing to lower closing costs. Your challenge is to find them. You may not know a good deal, however, unless you've thoroughly researched the market.

Everything on a mortgage is negotiable—regardless of what the institution advertises. This includes rates, points, prepayment penalties, etc. Each time you refinance, be prepared to shop around and to negotiate. You can almost always save a quarter of a percent if you open (or have) an account at the bank or savings and loan and arrange to have automatic payments debited from your bank account. But don't stop there. Another lender may have a rate below that, or the same rate with lower closing costs.

Prepayment Penalties

There is a clause in all mortgages relating to prepayment and what, if any, prepayment penalty is charged if you prepay before a certain date. The shorter the duration and/or the cheaper the prepayment penalty, the sooner you can take advantage of changing rates in the marketplace. Sometimes if you refinance with the same lender, they will waive the prepayment penalty. A mortgage with no prepayment penalty is best. If your lender insists on including a prepayment penalty, strive toward one that lasts no longer than two to three years.

Costs of Refinancing

The costs of refinancing are similar to closing costs, except that local/state taxes, if any, are not included. Costs for the following are negotiable and will vary considerably:

- Lender's attorney's review fees *(listed as a possible fee but rarely applied)*

- Title search and insurance *(negotiable)*

- Application fee *(varies considerably—includes credit check and other miscellaneous charges)*

- Appraisal fee *(varies considerably—some lenders have their own appraiser and do not charge; others have a list, and you can negotiate with anyone on the list)*

- Loan-origination fee or points *(try to avoid these—however, if it buys you a quarter-point reduction in interest below any other mortgage available, you will generally come out ahead)*

In analyzing your costs, lump everything together except the loan-origination fee or points. By now you have polled every possible mortgage lender and have identified who has the lowest interest rates. Now, holding the interest rates constant, look for the lowest closing costs. Begin negotiating between lenders. See if you can get one lender to beat the rates or costs of another lender. If it is a deposit institution, see if you can get them to cut the rate if you open an account and have direct payment of your mortgage. This saves you money and is a great convenience. Watch the real estate section of the paper religiously. Occasionally, a respectable lender will have to meet a sales target, particularly toward the end of a quarter.

Computing whether you should refinance based on cost is simple. Compute the monthly savings of the new mortgage. Take your total costs of refinancing, including points, and see how many months of savings will be used to pay back the costs. For example, the cost to refinance is $1,500. By refinancing you save $115 a month. $1,500/$115 = 13 months. It will take you 13 months to pay back the costs of refinancing. Thus, by refinancing you will save $115 a month for every month you live in the house after the first 13 months. If you live in the house for five years after you refinance, you will save $5,405.

Home-Equity Loans

Marty desperately needed money. One of his kids needed braces. The car was hobbling along on its last legs. While he could have taken out a personal loan to finance these expenditures, he had heard that he might be able to obtain a home-equity loan on better terms and he could get a tax deduction for the interest payments he made on the loan. He didn't like the idea of using his home to back the loan, though.

How Home-Equity Loans Work

Home-equity loans can take the form of either secured installment loans or secured lines of credit. Under a home-equity loan, your lending institution acquires a security interest in your home up to the amount of your loan. In the event of a default, you could lose your home. This is because your home serves as collateral for the loan. The principal danger with these loans is that credit limits are usually so high that families may increase their debt well beyond prudent levels. In doing so, they may substantially reduce their home equity, the principal savings for many households.

In recent years home-equity loans have become a very popular lending product. This is because after the 1986 federal tax-reform law, these loans have become one of the last remaining tax loopholes available to consumers. You are generally able to deduct interest expenses you pay on a home-equity loan (although certain exceptions do exist—see Chapter 14). If interest deductibility is important to you, consult with a tax adviser before applying for a home-equity loan.

New Home-Equity Loan Products

Many financial institutions are now vigorously advertising for home-equity loan business. Creative, new home-equity loan products, with varying features, are frequently emerging. Variable-interest home-equity loans abound; others come with fixed interest rates; some offer low monthly payments with balloon payments at the end of the loan. With some home-equity loans you can even write checks or use a credit card that accesses the equity you have in your home. Pre-approved lines of credit to your home's equity hold forth the promise of never having to apply for another loan.

Since products vary tremendously, you must carefully evaluate home-equity loan offerings. Shop around to find the loan that best suits your individual needs. If your borrowing needs are relatively small, you might consider pursuing a personal, unsecured loan or using savings instead. Do not apply for a home-equity loan if you are in any way irresponsible with money. The risks are simply too great to play around with the equity in your home.

Variable-Rate Home-Equity Loans

Almost all home-equity products are variable-interest loans, many of which appear to carry very low interest rates. Some of these are simply promotional rates, available through a certain date or for a set period of time (normally ninety days). Thereafter, the actual rate will usually be indexed to an outside rate, like the prime lending rate, with a specified percentage added. Thus, you may benefit from the promotional rate only for a short period of time, with the bulk of your loan coming at a substantially higher interest rate. This actual rate, however, may still be lower than anything else you can obtain on the market. Since your indebtedness is linked to an outside index, you might be subjected to higher or lower interest rates in the future.

If you take out a variable-rate home-equity loan, you should be wary of the uncertainties of changing economic conditions. Do not take out a long-term home-equity loan just on the off chance that interest rates will remain low. Should you obtain an open-end home-equity loan, do not use more of your approved line of credit than you can realistically repay in a couple of years. Or take out a short-term, closed-end loan of two to three years. Then if interest rates skyrocket, you should be able to pay off your obligations fairly quickly. If you need to borrow more money, you will be able to base your decision on the economic conditions of the time rather than being locked in to a high interest rate under a long-term loan.

If your loan has a variable-interest rate, check to see whether you are allowed to convert it to a fixed rate.

Costs of Home-Equity Loans

Home-equity loans carry the same sorts of expenses you would normally encounter when buying a house (closing costs, appraisal fees, title, points, attorney's fees). Other costs your lender attaches to the loan may include application fees, annual fees, transaction charges, prepayment penalties, and other service charges. In many instances, however, lenders may be willing to lower or possibly waive the closing costs. So shop around.

Many home-equity loans require relatively high minimum loan amounts, normally $5,000 or more. Some loans also carry maximum or minimum withdrawal requirements. In addition, lenders place an outside limit on the percentage of equity in your home you can access. Most lenders will allow you to borrow only around 75 to 80 percent of your home's current market value, minus any encumbrances (like your first mortgage or any second mortgages). If you just purchased a home, you may have very little equity built up. If you have your house almost paid for or are well into a long-term mortgage or made a considerable down payment, you may have considerable equity at your disposal.

The interest rates charged on home-equity loans are normally well below the interest rates charged on most other loan products (especially unsecured loans like credit cards and personal loans). The combination of lower rates and potential tax deductions make home-equity loans some of the most attractive loan products on the market today.

Second Mortgages

Edith needs to make some repairs to her home. She also has always wanted a sun room built onto the house, and she is now ready to build. She still has many years left on her first mortgage, which she got at a very favorable fixed rate. Edith wonders if she should consider a second mortgage instead of refinancing her entire mortgage or using a home-equity line of credit for the repairs and addition.

Why Obtain a Second Mortgage?

You would take a second mortgage loan instead of obtaining a home-equity loan if you needed a lump-sum loan that you expected to repay over a long period and/or wanted a fixed-interest-rate commitment. You would take a second mortgage rather than refinancing your existing mortgage if:

- Your first mortgage interest is substantially less than the available refinancing rate.

- The available second-mortgage rate is not substantially higher than the refinancing rate.

- The points you would pay to refinance the entire mortgage would increase your total interest cost above the combined interest costs of a first and second mortgage.

In Edith's situation, she currently owes $50,000 on a home valued at $100,000. Her mortgage has twenty-five years remaining, and her fixed rate is 5.5 percent. Edith needs $30,000 for the repairs and addition she wants to build. She has investigated and found that she can refinance at 7.5 percent for thirty years with two points. She also can obtain a 25-year second mortgage at 8 percent with two points. With either loan, Edith plans to roll the points into the loan and amortize their payment with the principal. The mortgage-initiation fees (other than the points) will be the same for both loans, so they will be ignored for the purposes of this comparison.

	Current Mortgage	Second Mortgage	First and Second Mortgage	Refinanced Mortgage
Payments	$307	$232	$539	$591
Amortized Points	N/A	$8	$8	$12
Total Payments	$307	$240	$547	$603

As you can see, under her particular circumstances, Edith is better off taking a second mortgage with slightly higher interest than the available refinancing rate and retaining her low-interest first mortgage. This strategy saves Edith $56 a month for twenty-five years, or a net savings of $16,800 over the twenty-five-year period ($9,580 in today's dollars assuming a 5 percent discount rate).

A second mortgage would not make sense if Edith's situation was slightly different. For example, if her current mortgage rate was 8 percent and refinancing was available for 7.5 percent with 2 points and second mortgages were available at 7.75 percent also with 2 points, the comparison would look like this:

	Current Mortgage	Second Mortgage	First and Second Mortgage	Refinanced Mortgage
Payments	$386	$227	$613	$591
Amortized Points	N/A	$8	$8	$12
Total Payments	$386	$235	$621	$603

Obtaining a Second Mortgage

You apply for a second mortgage in the same way you apply for refinancing. Your bank will require most or all of the same credit and appraisal information that is required for a refinancing. Income-to-debt ratios are the same as for refinancing. As mentioned earlier, your first and second mortgage total is usually limited to 80 percent of your home's value. The costs of obtaining a second mortgage will also be similar to refinancing.

The only real difference between refinancing and a second mortgage is that the interest rate may be higher. The higher rate is a premium payment the lender requires in order to make a riskier loan. A second mortgage is riskier than refinancing because the second mortgage is "subordinate" to the first mortgage. This means that if you default on your loan(s) and the house is sold to pay the debt, the first mortgage holder will be repaid first and whatever is left (up to the debt amount) will go to the second mortgage holder. Any amount in excess of the first and second mortgage will be given to the property owner, unless other debts were secured with the property.

For example, Edith defaults on her first and second mortgages, and her house is sold. Because real estate values have fallen and the house is in bad condition, it sells for only $82,000. Once real estate fees and settlement costs are deducted, the sale proceeds total $75,000. The first mortgage holder is paid in full ($50,000) and the second mortgage holder receives $25,000, losing $5,000 in principal.

Questions to Ask When Refinancing, Getting a Home-Equity Line, or Obtaining a Second Mortgage

When refinancing, getting a home-equity line of credit, or applying for a second mortgage, you should shop around to get the best rates and conditions. The following questions will help you compare lenders' terms and conditions. (Questions specific to home-equity loans are noted.)

INITIATION COSTS

- Is there an application fee? How much is it?

- Will an appraisal be required? How much will the appraisal cost?

- Will a title search be required? How much will the title search cost?

- How much will attorney fees run?

- Are there points? How much are they?

- Are there any other initiation costs? How much will they be?

RATES

- What is the annual percentage rate (APR) for fixed-interest loans?

- What is the variable APR for a variable-rate loan?

- Is there a promotional rate at the start of the loan? How is it calculated? How long does it last?

- How long are the periods for the variable-rate loan (i.e., how often does the rate adjust)?

- How much can the variable rate change in a period?

- Is there a maximum interest rate for the variable-rate loan (a cap)?

- What is the "worst-case" monthly payment for the variable-rate loan (i.e., the monthly payment at the highest possible rate)?

- Can the variable-rate loan be converted to a fixed rate? Are there restrictions on when and how it may be converted?

- What is the variable rate set by (i.e., what index is used)?

GENERAL LOAN CONDITIONS

- How much will you lend?

- How large is the credit line? (home equity)

- What is the loan term (length)? May I extend the term?

- Is there a penalty if you repay the loan before the term expires? What is the penalty?

- Are there late-payment charges? How much are they?

- Do the loan payments include principal and interest?

- Does the loan amortize completely over the loan term, or is there a balloon payment at the end of the term? May I refinance a balloon payment?

- Are there terms and conditions of the loan that can or will change during the loan?

- What conditions would put the loan in default? What conditions would require immediate repayment of the full loan amount?

- Is there a minimum first withdrawal? (home equity)

- May I withdraw as much as I like at a time, or are there minimums and maximums? (home equity)

- Are there minimum payment amounts? What are they? How are they calculated? (home equity)

- How do I access the home-equity credit line (checks, other)? (home equity)

CHAPTER 14

Tax Repercussions

Laura and Jim are currently living in a temporary home. In a year or so they may have to move. Laura wants to figure out if it will be cheaper to buy or rent a house. Some of her friends tell her she is crazy not to buy because of the tax advantages, but Laura is not so sure and wants to calculate the tax savings herself.

Owning a residence may or may not be cheaper than renting a comparable house or apartment (see Chapter 5 for discussion of renting versus owning). The tax advantage of home ownership (the tax savings provided by the mortgage-interest deduction from federal and most state income taxes) is one factor in the cost comparison. Other factors include:

- Maintenance costs
- Utility costs
- Property taxes
- Property and liability insurance
- Appreciation or depreciation of the property's value

Tax savings alone should never drive a decision to purchase. The total cost of ownership plus individual preferences should be the determining factors. This chapter will focus on calculating tax savings as part of the overall cost of home ownership.

Purpose of Mortgage-Interest Deduction

Simply put, the mortgage-interest deduction shelters the income you use to finance a home purchase from federal income tax. You are allowed to deduct the interest payments you make on your mortgage for your main and/or second home from your gross income, thereby reducing taxable income. The IRS defines mortgage interest as such:

> Generally, mortgage interest is any interest you pay on a loan secured by your home (main or a second home). These loans include: a mortgage to buy your home, a second mortgage, a line of credit, and a home-equity loan.

Remember, mortgage interest is not the total amount of your payment, but rather the payment amount less the principal portion of that payment.

The mortgage-interest deduction is provided by the federal government to encourage home ownership by reducing its cost. The federal government provides the tax deduction because it believes that home ownership creates more stable communities and provides citizens a savings vehicle that can lead to substantial equity (wealth) accumulation.

Rules Governing Deductibility

The rules governing deductibility of mortgage interest will make sense to you if you keep in mind that they are designed to assure that the mortgage-interest deduction is used solely for the purposes it was created for—to make ownership more affordable and to encourage equity accumulation. The rules governing mortgage-interest deductibility prevent the use of this deduction for other purposes by establishing three limits:

$1.1 Million Cumulative Mortgage-Debt Limit

Because ownership affordability is the first goal, the rules limit the interest deduction on "acquisition" debt (mortgage debt used to buy, build, or improve your home—including any home-equity loan funds used to improve your home substantially) to interest paid on mortgage debt totaling $1.0 million or less during the tax year. Interest deduction for "equity" debt (mortgage debt assumed for purposes other than to buy, build, or improve your home) is limited to debt totaling $100,000 or less during the tax year (see following section for complete definition of acquisition and equity debt). These rules were instituted on October 13, 1987, and apply to new mortgages. Mortgage debt incurred before October 13, 1987, is "grandfathered" and is not subject to these limits. If you have a grandfathered mortgage and want to assume additional mortgage debt, the mortgage-interest deduction limits for the new debt will be calculated on the combined balance of grandfathered and new debt.

The acquisition and equity limits apply to the cumulative mortgage debt that you owe on your main residence (the home you live in most of the time) and/or a second home. Persons assuming acquisition and equity mortgage obligations in excess of $1.1 million on their main and/or second home are not believed to need additional interest deductions to enhance affordability.

The $1.1 million cumulative mortgage-debt limit ($1.0 million in acquisition debt and $100,000 in equity debt) applies to outstanding balances and is not limited by mortgage principal repaid in the past. As you pay off mortgage debt, you can add that amount back into your available mortgage limits. For example, if you currently owed $350,000 on a $400,000 mortgage for your main residence, $100,000 on a $200,000 mortgage for your beach house, and $50,000 on a $100,000 home-equity loan—you are currently deducting mortgage interest on $500,000 of principal. This means that you could deduct interest on an additional $550,000 in acquisition debt and $50,000 in equity debt if you chose to assume additional debt.

Limitation on Mortgage Purpose

Because affordable home ownership is the societal purpose served by the mortgage-interest deduction, the rules are designed to prevent the use of this deduction to finance expenditures unrelated to the goal of ownership (e.g., using the proceeds from a refinancing, second-mortgage, or home-equity loan to finance a new business, vacation, new car purchase, or other purposes unrelated to the purchase, construction, or improvement of your main or second home). An exception to this principle is a rule allowing persons to use up to $100,000 of their home equity (through a second mortgage or home-equity loan) for purposes other than renovations and still deduct the interest on the loan from their taxable income.

Equity/Second Mortgage Borrowing Limits

Because equity accumulation is another goal of the mortgage-interest deduction policy, the rules strictly regulate the deductibility of interest paid on home-equity loans and second mortgages. As mentioned earlier, you may deduct the interest on home-equity loans and second mortgages in any amount (up to your total acquisition debt limit of $1 million) if those loans are used for additions or substantial improvements to your home. This is allowed because you are increasing the value of your home.

You may also deduct the interest on up to $100,000 in a home-equity loan or a second mortgage obtained for purposes unrelated to home purchase, construction, or improvements. This $100,000 home-equity/second-mortgage provision is an exception to the goals of the mortgage-interest deduction and may best be explained as a concession to the political power of homeowners.

Limits of Mortgage-Interest Deductions by Debt Type

Acquisition Debt

Acquisition debt is debt you incur to purchase, build, or substantially improve (renovate or add) to your main or second home. Acquisition debt may be in the form of a first or second mortgage, or a home-equity loan. The type and/or name of the loan does not determine whether it is acquisition debt but rather the purpose the loan is used for.

Currently, the IRS definition for the deductibility of mortgage interest associated with acquisition debt is: "Mortgages you took out after October 13, 1987, to buy, build, or improve your home (called home acquisition debt), but only if these mortgages totaled $1 million or less [throughout the tax year]." Loans made on or before October 13, 1987, are subject to different rules (see IRS publication 936: Home Mortgage Interest Deduction for details).

Equity Debt

Equity is the part of the home value that belongs to the owner, not to lenders. Equity may be calculated as the difference between a home's value and any loans owed on the home. (Example: A condominium is valued at $85,000 and the owner has a $30,000 mortgage and a $10,000 second mortgage. The cumulative debt on the condominium is $40,000, leaving $45,000 in equity.)

Equity debt, however, for the purposes of tax deductibility is not simply debt you assume using your home's equity as collateral. Rather, its IRS definition is: "mortgages you took out after October 13, 1987, other than to buy, build, or improve your home (called home equity debt), but only if these mortgages totaled $100,000 or less [throughout the tax year]."

Second Mortgages

A second mortgage is a loan you assume in addition to your first (existing) mortgage that is made to you using your home as collateral. Second mortgages allow you to take equity out of your property without disturbing or refinancing the original mortgage. The interest on a second mortgage is tax-deductible if the loan proceeds are used to substantially improve or add on to the residence (e.g., a kitchen renovation or family room addition). If the second mortgage (or a portion of it) is used for purposes unrelated to additions or improvements, your interest deduction on the debt unrelated to home improvements is limited to debts totaling $100,000 or less.

Refinancing

Refinancing a mortgage means to replace the current mortgage with a new one. Refinancing allows you to (1) gain better terms (lower interest rate, longer/shorter amortization, etc.); (2) increase your debt on the property in order to remove accumulated equity; or (3) gain better terms and increase your debt. The interest on a refinanced mortgage will receive one of several tax treatments depending on previous debt and how you use the proceeds:

1. If the mortgage is grandfathered (made on or before October 13, 1987) and you are refinancing for an amount not more than the outstanding balance, the refinanced mortgage continues to be treated as grandfathered debt, and the interest is fully deductible regardless of the principal amount.
2. If the mortgage is grandfathered and you refinance for more than the outstanding principal, the portion of the mortgage that equals the outstanding principal is treated as grandfathered debt and the excess is treated as new.
3. If the mortgage is not grandfathered, the principal is not increased, and the new mortgage complies with the

$1 million acquisition-debt limit, the interest is fully deductible.

4. If the mortgage is not grandfathered, the mortgage principal is increased to substantially improve or add on to a main or second home, and the new principal amount is less than the $1 million acquisition-debt limit, the mortgage interest is fully deductible.

5. If the debt amount is increased, and the increased amount is used for purposes other than substantial improvements or additions to a main or second home:

   - The interest on the portion of the new loan equal to the pre-refinancing mortgage balance remains deductible in the new mortgage

   - The interest on the new debt (up to $100,000) is fully deductible

   - The interest on any new debt in excess of $100,000 is not deductible

Suppose you bought your house in 1980 with a thirty-year mortgage of $100,000 at 8 percent. In 1995, you needed money for your children's education and decided to use $50,000 of your home equity for this purpose. To do this, you refinanced your mortgage, adding $50,000 to the outstanding balance of $77,000, for a total of $127,000. You will be able to deduct the interest you pay on the new mortgage balance of $127,000.

Tax Issues Related to Mortgage Initiation and Home Purchase

Points Deductibility

"Points" are charges you or the seller pays to obtain your mortgage. Points are often called origination fees, discount points, or loan charges. The dollar value of the points you pay for your acquisition mortgage (the original mortgage you take to finance your purchase) on your *principal* residence (and the value of any points the seller pays for you at closing) may be deducted in full from your taxable income in the year you purchase your home if the following conditions are met:

- Paying points is a typical practice in your area.

- The points paid were not more than the typical points charged in the area.

- You use the "cash method" of accounting (reporting income in the year you earn it and deducting expenses in the year they occur—most people use this method).

- The points were calculated as a percentage of the mortgage amount.

- The points were not paid in lieu of "closing cost" expenses (e.g., appraisal fees, attorney fees, etc.) or property taxes.

- The points are clearly shown on settlement forms as points paid in connection with the mortgage.

- The points deducted were not more than the funds you actually provided out-of-pocket at the closing (i.e., the points may not be financed by your lender or mortgage broker). The "funds" do not have to have been paid specifically to points, may have been paid for a down payment, closing costs, or for any purpose at the closing. See IRS publication 936 for further information and examples.

In contrast, the points you pay to purchase a *second home* (e.g., vacation home) or to *refinance* a mortgage must be amortized (divided equally) and deducted over the term of the refinancing with only one exception: if you pay points for refinancing a mortgage, and part of the money you receive as a result of refinancing is used to pay for qualifying home improvements on your *main* residence (consult the IRS for specific guidance on which home improvements will qualify), points paid on these funds may be deducted in full in the year of the refinancing.

This means that if you refinance $100,000 for thirty years, pay $3,000 in points, and use $50,000 for qualifying home improvements, $1,500 of the points may be deducted from your taxable income that year and $50 may be deducted each year for thirty years. Should you pay off the refinancing before the amortization is complete, you may deduct the remaining balance of the points in the year that you pay off the loan.

Refunds of Interest

If you receive an interest refund associated with your mortgage payments for any reason, you must adjust your interest deduction to reflect this event. This means that if you receive the refund in the year that you paid the interest, you must adjust the interest deduction you are claiming that year by the refunded amount. If the refund is for interest paid in a previous year, generally you will include the interest in your income in the year the refund was received.

Closing Costs

The costs you pay at closing or settlement (e.g., real estate commissions, attorney fees, appraisal fees, transfer taxes, document-preparations fees, recording fees, etc.) are considered by the IRS to be "capital expenses." You cannot deduct these costs under your mortgage-interest deduction. Rather, these expenses are added to your home's "basis," the amount you have paid to purchase and improve your home, reducing any capital gains exposure you may have when selling your home if it has appreciated.

Property Taxes Paid by Seller

Any advance payment of property taxes that the seller has made on your home in the year of purchase may be deducted from your taxable income that year. An example would be if a seller has prepaid $4,000 for the full year's property taxes and you buy the house on July 1. In this scenario, you may deduct $2,000 in property taxes from your income that year, even though you did not directly pay the property tax bill. You may do this because the prepayment is assumed to be passed along in the purchase price.

Capital Gains Taxes When You Sell Your Home

In general, you will pay taxes on the capital gains from the sale of your home unless you buy another home of equal or greater value within two years. Capital gain or loss is defined as the difference between the amount realized from the sale (i.e., selling price less selling expenses) minus the adjusted basis of your home (i.e., the original sale price plus allowable closing costs from the purchase and any capital improvements, less all depreciation claimed).

If you or your spouse are fifty-five or older and have owned and lived in your main home for at least three of the five years preceding the sale, you may exempt the first $125,000 of capital gains related to the sale of your main residence from capital gains taxes if you buy a less expensive home or do not buy another home. The capital gains exemption for homeowners over fifty-five is a one-time exemption—use it carefully!

Calculating the Tax Savings of Home Ownership

Here's an example. Bert did not own a home in 1994. His 1994 "total income" reported on his 1040 form was $53,000. He itemized his deductions, subtracting $4,400 from this income for state and local taxes (instead of the $3,800 standard deduction for a single person). He also deducted $2,450 for his one personal exemption. This left him a taxable income of $46,150 and a total federal tax liability of $9,958, representing a federal tax rate of 21.6 percent on his taxable income or federal tax rate of 18.8 percent on his "total income."

Note: Bert's average tax rate of 21.6 percent differs from the standard (or marginal) rates of 15, 28, 31, 36, and 39.5 percent because portions of your income are subjected to different standard rates (e.g., the first $23,350 of a single person's taxable income is taxed at 15 percent, the next $33,200 of taxable income is taxed at 28 percent, etc.) causing you to have an "average rate" somewhere in between.

If Bert had bought a $100,000 condominium at the first of the year and acquired a $90,000, no-points mortgage for thirty years at a fixed interest rate of 9 percent, he would have made monthly mortgage payments of $724 in 1994. Of the $8,688 ($724 × 12 months) Bert would have paid for his mortgage in 1994, $8,073 of the payments would have been for interest and $615 would have gone to principal repayment. The interest portion of the mortgage payment would have been deductible from Bert's federal taxable income, lowering his federal taxable income from $46,150 to $38,077. (Mortgage interest is also deductible from most state income tax calculations, providing further savings. The rules governing mortgage-interest deductibility from taxable state income vary by state.)

The 1994 federal taxes on Bert's $38,077 taxable income (after the mortgage-interest deduction) would have been $7,704, for a tax savings of $2,254 ($9,958 − $7,704). (Bert's state income tax obligation would also have been reduced, although as mentioned above, exact savings varies by state.)

Buying the condominium would have saved Bert the 28 percent federal taxes he paid on the $8,073 of taxable income that he could have paid for mortgage interest. The tax savings is 28 percent because the $8,073 Bert would have deducted for mortgage interest would be deducted from the portion of his income that was taxed at the highest incremental rate. (Bert would also have saved 5 percent to 9 percent on the state taxes that he paid on the same $8,073 of income.)

The interest you pay on a mortgage on your main and/or second home is tax-deductible. This interest deduction applies to combined mortgages of $1 million in acquisition debt and

$100,000 in equity debt unrelated to home improvements. This means that you do not pay federal income tax on the income you use to pay the *interest* on a qualifying first mortgage, second mortgage, or home-equity loans. You do pay tax on the income used to pay the principal portion of each payment. Principal payments are typically a relatively small percentage of the monthly payment in the early years of any of these loans. For example, in the first year of your mortgage, the mortgage payment you make on a $100,000, thirty-year fixed mortgage at 8 percent would be $734 per month, or $8,008 for the year. However, the interest portion of your mortgage payment would be slightly less than the total payment because some of each payment goes to repaying the principal. In the first year of this mortgage, you repay approximately $70 of principal a month, for a total of $835 for the year. This means that the interest portion of your payments would equal the total payments ($8,008) less the principal repayment ($835) or $7,173. In the first year of your mortgage, $7,173 would be your allowable mortgage-interest deduction. In the fifteenth year of your mortgage your mortgage payments would still total $8,008, but your principal payments will have grown to $2,550 per year, causing the deductible mortgage-interest portion of your payments to fall to $5,458.

Calculating your potential tax savings is relatively easy. You will need the following information to fill in the work sheet that follows:

Your Tax Rate

To calculate your tax savings you may do one of two things:

1. Consult a tax specialist or the IRS for the highest marginal tax rate you paid last year (based on your taxable income). Your highest marginal rate (15, 28, 31, 36, or 39.5 percent) is the tax rate you should use because the income you deduct for mortgage-interest payments will "come off the top" of your taxable income.
2. Use a rougher estimate of your combined (or average tax rate), calculated by dividing the federal tax you paid last

year by your gross income (pre-tax income) from last year. If you expect your income to change dramatically in the year you purchase or in the next several years, estimate your new tax rate by recalculating your taxes from last year.

Your Yearly Interest Payments

The interest payments you will make on your projected mortgage are calculated by deducting the first year's principal repayment amount from the twelve-month payment total. If you do not know how to calculate these two figures, ask your mortgage banker to help or use the full twelve-month payment amount for this calculation (it will be quite close to the actual figure).

Calculation Worksheet for Tax Savings

Use the following worksheet to estimate your *first year* federal tax savings due to the mortgage-interest deduction. Remember that the tax savings from the mortgage-interest deduction will diminish slightly each year as the interest portion of your payment falls and the principal portion increases.

Please note that the following worksheet uses the total of your mortgage payments in the first year as an estimate of the mortgage interest you will pay. This is done because the amounts will be very close in the first year and because the interest calculation is far more complex. For a more accurate estimate, ask your mortgage broker to calculate the exact interest you will pay in the first year.

The worksheet also assumes that the federal tax rates and exemptions have not changed between your last year's return and this year's. If federal tax rules have changed, you should consult a tax accountant for the impact the new rules will have on the mortgage-interest deduction.

The worksheet gives an example for each calculation. The example calculations are derived from the example at the start of this chapter (Bert's calculations).

Task	Calculation	Example Calculation	Answer
1. Calculate last year's federal tax rate	Consult a tax specialist or the IRS for your highest marginal rate (based on your taxable income from last year) or make a rough calculation by dividing your federal taxes paid last year by your taxable income (income after deductions)	$9,958 ÷ $46,150	.2157 or 21.6%
2. Calculate monthly mortgage-interest payments for the first year of the mortgage	Calculate your monthly mortgage amount using the table in Chapter 5	$8.05 × 90 ($1,000 at 9% for 30 years = $8.05/ mo.)	$724.50
3. Calculate the yearly mortgage-interest payment for the first year of the mortgage	Multiply the monthly payment amount (from task 2) by 12	$724.50 × 12	$8,694

Task	Calculation	Example Calculation	Answer
4. Calculate the tax savings accruing directly from the mortgage-interest deduction	Multiply the yearly mortgage interest amount (from task 3) by your federal tax rate	$8,694 × .216	$1,877
5. Calculate the total tax savings accruing from the mortgage-interest deduction	Review your last year's federal tax form and recalculate the payment due after the mortgage deduction. Subtract this payment amount from the tax payment you made. If this amount is more than the amount calculated in task 4, then the deduction caused you to move into a lower federal tax bracket, saving you additional money	$9,958 − $7,704	$2,254

Note: If your first or second mortgage balance or your home-equity balance exceeds the limits discussed at the start of this chapter, use the interest payments on the maximum allowable balances for the calculations.

Work Space

CHAPTER 15

Managing Your Mortgage

After weeks of going back and forth with a lender, Marion's loan was finally approved. She breathed a sigh of relief, thinking that she'd never have to worry about mortgage-related issues ever again.

Soon after obtaining her mortgage, Liz was surprised to get something in the mail saying that her mortgage had been transferred to another lender. She was curious as to what was going on.

Assume your mortgage-loan application has been approved, you've gone to closing, and you've moved into your new home. Now can you forget about mortgage-related issues for the foreseeable future?

The answer is no. Up until this point you have probably focused considerable attention on and devoted financial resources into your commitment to home ownership. You've developed the financial resources to cough up a significant amount for a down payment on your first home or for a larger one. You've spent a lot of time and effort on developing a favorable record or basis for a lender to take a chance with you and give you that all-important mortgage. You're probably quite relieved that you've weathered the trials and tribulations of finding a house, qualifying for a mortgage, and finally making it to closing.

As a new homeowner, though, there are several things you need to be familiar with. First, you need to keep an eye on interest rates and check out any hot new mortgage products that may be better than the deal you've just struck. Chances are pretty good that you'll stick with what you've got. But there's always the possibility that something new and improved will come along that you'll obviously want to find out more about to determine whether it's worth your while to get a new mortgage. If you've learned anything from this book, it's that you should shop around—whether you've currently got a mortgage that you can do better on or need to find a mortgage initially.

In addition to continuing to shop around, you also need to understand at the outset the new responsibilities that have been conferred on you because you are a homeowner. It's very important that you understand your obligations and keep current on any mortgage-related expenses you may incur. You may encounter costs relating to home ownership for repairs, dwelling insurance, property taxes, co-op or condo fees, and some unexpected matters that you may not have contemplated. Indeed, you may have rented before buying and never really even had to worry about calling a plumber if something leaked, or having an exterminator in to kill roaches. Maybe you lived at home, where your parents took care of all of these things. Such matters represent financial responsibilities that you must now assume. As a result, you need to be financially prepared to respond to whatever house-related emergencies and expenses come along.

What's more, your house probably represents a significant area of savings for you. As a result, you need to keep it in as good a condition as possible to protect your investment. If it falls into disrepair, the value of your property may decline.

You also have a great deal to lose if you become delinquent or default on the financial obligations you committed yourself to in your mortgage contract. The failure to make timely payments as agreed upon could result in loss of your home, and you could wind up out on the street. So it's very important that you make every effort to remain current on your mortgage and home-related expenses so they do not get away from you.

In addition, there is a very good chance that your original lender will sell your mortgage in the secondary market. This means that even though you negotiated your mortgage contract with a particular lender, someone else will probably wind up "holding" or "owning" your mortgage. In fact, throughout your loan, several different lenders may own it. While these different ownerships will not change the terms of your contractual agreement, you need to understand what to expect when and if your original lender sells your mortgage loan to someone else.

Plan Ahead for the Unexpected

You may recall that in Chapter 2, it was suggested that you develop a financial goal of socking away about six months of your take-home pay into a short-term savings nest egg. You may have thought that goal was somewhat unrealistic given the fact that you had a difficult time coming up with the required down payment for your home. Be that as it may, there are some very compelling reasons for creating a savings slush fund or stashing away some "mad money." One of the best reasons for this can be summed up in two little words: home repairs.

While some repairs can be anticipated, others cannot, and you may have little or no control over home-repair crises that arise. A cantankerous water heater or furnace may suddenly decide to shut down after years of faithful service to the previous owner. The roof may spring a leak that damages some of your furnishings while destroying a wall, ceiling, and some flooring. Condos or co-ops may suddenly require major structural repairs.

Ironically, many home repairs hit you at the most inopportune moments. For example, the air conditioning goes kaput not at the end of the summer but at the beginning of it, during the biggest heat wave of the century. Or you wind up with plumbing problems the same week you're preparing your annual income tax return and are already reeling over how much you owe in taxes.

While responding to unexpected expenses needs to be taken into consideration, you probably have lots of other home-related expenses. Most people aren't like a friend of mine who stockpiled expensive furniture in his one-bedroom apartment in anticipation of the day he'd finally buy a home. There was barely room to walk around all of the furniture he had purchased for use in the home he would someday purchase. Well, when that day finally arrived, he bought a beautiful two-bedroom unit with lots of space. In spite of my friend's best-laid plans, he needed to buy a lot more furniture to fill his new pad. Some of his planning did pay off because he was ahead of the curve in purchasing home furnishings. Other people are not so lucky.

If you buy a house, you may need to landscape the yard, replace overgrown shrubs, or disinter a hideous rock garden the previous owner was particularly fond of. You may need to redecorate. Maybe you don't like the "harvest gold" appliances in the kitchen. Perhaps the previous owner's decorating mantra was "don't be afraid of color." The only problem is, you can't stand the thought of a sunshine yellow kitchen or a Chinese red bedroom. You might hate the carpet or floor covering and want to select something more in tune with your tastes that'll go with your furniture.

In order to respond to these exigencies, you need to plan ahead. Develop a new household budget that takes the increased cost of home ownership into consideration. Develop a savings plan to create a "home maintenance account" where you place money and specifically earmark it for home-related expenses, including both routine maintenance and major repairs.

You also need to think about the "unthinkable." You could be involved in an accident; a member of your immediate family could be stricken with an illness; you could lose your job or experience a reduction in pay; you and your spouse could become separated or decide to divorce. Not knowing what the future holds, you need to plan for the unexpected.

Savings is the best way of insulating yourself from harm should any of the above events occur. Needless to say, it is far easier to respond to these events if you plan ahead before you are under considerable stress and strain and dealing with highly emotional and traumatic events in your life. In such cases you probably need to devote yourself to responding to the problem at hand rather than worrying about whether they are going to cause you to lose your home.

Since you just assumed a significant amount of debt in obtaining your mortgage, you need to make sure you're going to be able to handle your mortgage obligations before you assume any new debt. As a result, you probably don't want to have to borrow money to accomplish routine repairs or to place them on a credit card with a high interest rate that may consume access to credit you may need for other things. If you have to borrow money to accomplish major repairs or improvements, try to refinance these on as favorable terms as possible. Would a second-mortgage or home-equity loan make sense? If you have not yet amassed sufficient equity in your home, you may be relegated to an installment loan. If you must finance these expenditures, shop around for the best interest rates on the loan you ultimately receive, just as you shopped around for your mortgage.

Staying Current on Your Mortgage

Your mortgage contract will spell out the financial obligations you are assuming. In exchange for the lender's money, you agreed to make monthly payments in the amount of $_____ on a certain date or on certain dates each month. Since this is the date your mortgage payment is due, make every effort to get your payment in on time. If you mail your payments, take into consideration a reasonable amount of time for your payment to reach its destination.

One of the easiest ways to assure your payments are made on time is to have your mortgage payments automatically deducted from your banking account. If your mortgage is with the same institution where you have your bank account, you may even have qualified for a discount on your mortgage if you agreed to have payments automatically deducted.

Suppose you get your payment in after the due date? Well, if it's pretty close to the due date, say a day or two late, nothing may happen. The lender may accept it anyway. Your payment, however, will probably be considered by the lender as having been received "late." Many lenders give homeowners a grace period ranging from a couple to as many as fifteen days or more after the due date to get their payments in before they're assessed a late fee. This obviously varies by lender. So, if you're going to be late on a payment, call your lender to determine its policy for collecting late-payment fees. Then try to get your payment to the lender before the date on which this fee will be levied.

If you find that you've fallen a couple of months behind on your mortgage payments, call the lender immediately to work out a specific plan for bringing your loan current. Most lenders do *not* want to foreclose on or refer your loan to collection agencies or attorneys to receive their payments. Given this, it's in your best interest to contact the lender immediately at the first sign of any payment glitches to avert any problems later on. Most lenders are willing to work with you to help you see yourself through any payment problems you are experiencing, particularly if you've taken the time and effort to let them know what's going on.

If you've missed three or more of your mortgage payments, your loan may be referred to an attorney or agency for collection, or foreclosure proceedings may be initiated against you. In such cases your entire loan may be declared due and immediately payable. This is because most mortgage contracts contain what is known as an "acceleration clause," which allows the lender to consider the entire loan due and immediately payable in the event of a default. The chances are pretty good that if you've been having trouble making a couple of scheduled payments, you probably don't have the financial resources to pay off your loan balance. You may also discover that you're liable for any attorney fees the lender may incur in its efforts to collect on your account. This is in addition to the money you may have to pay to an attorney to represent you. Again, a provision was probably included in your contract under which you're obliged to pay your lender's attorney fees.

Given all of these circumstances, it's in your best interest to keep things from going this far. Work with your lender. Open up lines of communication at the first sign of trouble. Keep the dialogue between you and the lender going. The absolute worst thing you could do if you're in default is avoid your lender. Rest assured, your lender has too much invested in you and your home to let non-payment languish for too long.

Normally, the willingness of your lender to work with you to overcome repayment problems bears some correlation to your past repayment history. If you've been diligent in making your mortgage payments for a considerable period of time and repayment problems represent an aberration, your lender will probably be more than willing to work with you. If, however, your past repayment efforts have been sporadic or if your lender has had to engage in efforts to get you to make your payments, you may have more difficulty. Because of this, it's best for you to make every effort to stay current on your obligations. This fact could come to your assistance should you encounter repayment problems later on.

If you are a couple of months or more behind in your mortgage payments, you'll probably need to agree with your lender upon a "mortgage workout plan." This agreement, which may be oral or in writing, specifically delineates how your mortgage problems will be resolved and how your payments will be brought up-to-date. The purpose of a workout plan is simple: to allow you to stay in your home and to avoid foreclosure.

If you're suffering from a temporary default that you'll likely to able to resolve in a month or two, your lender may grant you a "temporary indulgence." An example of circumstances wherein such an indulgence might be granted is when your home has been damaged by fire and you're waiting for an insurance payment. Here, your lender would probably want to see a copy of your insurance contract and any damage appraisals or letters of commitment you have received from your insurer. Based on this, your lender may be able to see that there is a reasonable expectation of payment in the foreseeable future or by a particular date.

Suppose you've gotten behind on your payments because you lost your job due to staffing reductions at your former place of employment. Now you've found another job that pays you more than your previous position. Under these circumstances you and your lender may work out a "repayment plan" under which you will not only make your future monthly mortgage payments when due, but you'll also make additional payments over a specific time period (maybe over a couple of years) to bring your missed payments current. Or you may have to make a commitment to make a lump-sum payment at a date certain.

What if you can't make any payments at all for a considerable length of time? Again, if you have a good track record with the lender, you may be able to work something out. Your lender may be willing to negotiate a "forbearance plan" under which you are either allowed to suspend your payments for a certain period of time or you will be able to make diminished payments (something less than your normal monthly payment). Of varying lengths, most forbearance plans normally last no longer than about a year and a half.

Obviously, your primary goal is to remain current on your mortgage payments and avoid having to develop a mortgage-workout plan with your lender. The options discussed above should be viewed solely as last-ditch alternatives to keep you in your house and avoid foreclosure.

Loan Transfers from One Lender to Another

Suppose you mail your monthly payments to a particular lender. In response, this lender takes your payments and makes insurance and tax payments on your behalf. If you have any problems or need some questions about your mortgage answered, you contact this same lender. Through all of these activities your lender is "servicing" your mortgage.

The fact of the matter is that a host of financial-service providers can function to "service" mortgage agreements. Your lender may originate as well as service the mortgage contracts it writes. In such cases it may be difficult to distinguish between the two functions. Many mortgage lenders either do not service the agreements they write or choose to sell or transfer servicing responsibilities to someone else.

This may happen at almost any time during the existence of your loan. The firm servicing your agreement may change hands several times during the life of your loan. Believe it or not, it may even happen right after you get the loan. While you may be required to make payments to a firm you may never have heard of before and to mail your payments to a distant state, the fact that your loan servicing has been sold is really no cause for alarm. You can rest assured that while the mechanics of how and where you make your payments may have changed, the basic contractual terms and conditions of your agreement (like the amount financed, interest rate, and other pricing components) will remain the same. That's because these terms "run" with the agreement, irrespective of who is servicing it.

The servicing of your mortgage loan can occur without your permission. Should this happen, your lender should notify you of this event at least fifteen days before your next monthly payment is due. This correspondence should alert you to: the fact that a transfer has occurred; the name, address, and telephone number of the new company that will be servicing your mortgage contract; the new payment mailing address; instructions for making future payments; and any other relevant information. You should also probably receive a similar letter from the new servicer of your contract detailing the same information.

If your mortgage-loan servicing is transferred, pay close attention to the information provided above. Do not continue to make payments to your old servicer. Once your contract has been transferred, your original lender will no longer be able to accept your payments, which they'll probably forward to the new servicer. This could result in a delay that would make your payment late. Your payment might even be lost. Since you don't want to be subjected to these sorts of events, make certain to make all future payments to the new servicer.

Some things may change. The new servicer may provide you with a new coupon book and ask you to discard the one you have been using. If you authorized automatic payments to your previous mortgage servicer, you will probably need to cancel this authorization and accomplish a new one with your new servicer identified as the recipient for all future payments. Since you may be unable to accomplish all of this within the same month, you may need to manually make your monthly payments for a month or two until your automatic-payment instructions take effect.

All collateral agreements relating to the servicing of your mortgage should also be transferred. For example, if your original agreement created a mortgage escrow account to cover insurance and tax payments, your old mortgage servicer should notify all relevant parties (e.g., the insurance company, local tax authority) of this change in financial arrangements. The old servicer should also notify the new servicer of the existence of such agreements.

Sometimes, however, things fall through the cracks. If you get a bill for insurance or tax payments that are supposed to be handled under your escrow agreement with your original agreement, check with the new servicer to make sure it knows of such escrow agreements.

You should also receive year-end interest payment notices from one or both of the lenders who serviced your loan during the course of the tax year in question. The lender to whom your original loan agreement has been transferred may provide you with a cumulative tax statement covering the entire year. This will be all-inclusive and reflect interest paid to both lenders during the portion of the year that each serviced your loan. Or you may receive separate tax statements from each lender reflecting the interest paid during the period of time during the tax year that each held your loan.

Should you encounter any problems after the loan has been transferred, you should contact the lender to whom your contract has been transferred. Your old lender may not be able to help because your files have been transferred or purged. In some instances, servicing responsibilities are transferred because a particular lender has merged with another lender or because a lender went out of business. Remember, once a transfer has taken place, the new servicer should become the entity with which most of your future interaction will occur. Your relationship with the original lender will have terminated upon transfer.

CHAPTER 16

Rejected Mortgage Applications

Maude worked long and hard to present a favorable impression on several prospective mortgage lenders. After months of exhausting searches and amassing gobs of information about herself and her past financial activities, she cannot find a mortgage lender who'll give her a loan. She's tired of this and wants to know how can she make sure this doesn't happen again.

What a crushing blow. After putting forth a great deal of effort and investing a considerable amount of time filling out an application, meeting with the prospective lender, and providing information that seemingly corroborates your very existence, your mortgage-loan application was rejected.

While it may be difficult to envision, you need to take steps to turn this negative into a positive in your life. For example, you've probably been put on notice about a factor or two that makes you financially unattractive. Maybe you've got a bad track record with other financial obligations that's reflected in negative entries on your credit report. Maybe you have too much outstanding debt. It could be that you don't have sufficient income or steady enough income to support the loan amount you requested. It could have been the property you sought to purchase. The appraised value could have been too low; the amount of the loan didn't support the value of the property being bought.

If your loan application has been rejected, don't despair. Instead, use the information you've learned about yourself and your financial condition to prepare yourself for a more favorable response the next time you apply for a mortgage loan.

Loan Appraisals

In some instances the appraised value on the property you wish to purchase may not meet lender requirements. Typically this occurs when the appraised value is below the purchase price. When this happens, the mortgage amount required to satisfy the contract price ends up representing a greater portion of the appraised value than most mortgage-underwriting standards will allow.

For example, assume the contract price for your house is $100,000 and the bank requires a 20 percent down payment. You are prepared to put $20,000 down and need an $80,000 mortgage. The appraised value of the house, however, comes in at $90,000. Unfortunately, the lender will calculate the 80 percent mortgage she is willing to loan based on the appraised value, only approving a $72,000 mortgage for the home. This will leave you with an $8,000 gap between your down payment and mortgage and the purchase price of the home.

If the home you are purchasing fails to appraise at the contract price, your first response (before the loan is actually rejected) should be to verify the validity of the appraisal. Did it reflect the changing nature of the neighborhood? Were the values of comparable houses in the same area with similar improvements factored into the appraiser's judgment?

You needn't be satisfied with a single appraiser's judgment. If you feel the appraised value is incorrect, have the property re-appraised by somebody else. If, however, the results of a second appraisal come in at close to the same estimate as the initial appraisal, you may need to reevaluate your position. If you are confronted with this circumstance, you have several options to consider:

1. Contact the seller of the property to see if he or she would be willing to lower the purchase price to the appraised value. In the example above, the seller would need to lower the sale price by $10,000. The seller may or may not be willing to do this. It depends on how long the property has been on the market and how anxious he or she is to sell.

2. Find out from the lender the maximum loan amount that it will approve on the property and decide if you want to increase your down payment to make up the difference between what the lender will loan and the agreed-upon purchase price. In the example above, you would have to increase your down payment from $20,000 to $28,000. This option may not be realistic since it requires a more substantial down payment than you may be able to afford.

3. If the appraisal is low due to certain repairs that are required to bring the house up to the necessary value, negotiate with the owner to have him or her make the repairs.

4. If you cannot renegotiate the price of the house or the estimated value determined by the appraiser, and do not want to pay the additional amount required to close the gap between the contract price and the maximum loan amount, you may exercise the financing contingency to void the contract. Although this would be disappointing, you might consider yourself fortunate to be released from buying a house that seems to be worth less than what you offered to pay.

Inadequate Money Available for Down Payment and Closing Costs

Another reason your loan application may be rejected is that the lender does not believe you have sufficient financial resources to make the down payment and meet closing costs. That's why it's very important to follow the steps outlined at the beginning of this book to prepare yourself for home ownership by developing a savings plan to meet these expenses when you finally get to this stage of the mortgage-application process. If you do not have enough money available, however, consider pursuing the following actions.

Contact the seller to see whether he or she will pay some or all of the closing costs. This step will obviously adversely impact the value of the sale from the seller's perspective. If the seller is willing to do this, however, it will reduce your initial financial outlays and may make the amount required to put you in a home closer within your reach.

Another option is to ask the seller to loan you the money to cover the down payment and closing costs in the form of a second mortgage between you and the seller. This, however, will be factored into your existing debt load by the lender when reviewing your application. Because of this additional indebtedness, the lender may not feel you'd be able to stay current on your loan payments on the original mortgage. Indeed, it might be difficult for you to make not only your mortgage payments to the primary lender but the payments on the second mortgage to the seller all at the same time. What's more, you are essentially borrowing money for the down payment, which will substantially increase the price you pay for your home. Should you decide to pursue this approach, make every effort to get the second mortgage on as favorable terms as possible and to repay it quickly to reduce your mortgage-related costs.

You might also consider forgoing your plans for immediate home ownership, establishing a savings plan to meet a down payment and closing costs, and waiting a while until you have accumulated the necessary financial resources.

Insufficient Income/Too Much Debt

Lenders will reject your mortgage application if they feel you may not be able to make your monthly mortgage payments easily. They worry that if you are stretched too thin financially, a financial setback (e.g., a layoff, job furlough, unexpected medical bills), even a small one, could cause you to fall behind on your payments and eventually default on the mortgage. A lender's worst fear is to have to go through the long, expensive, and emotionally draining process of foreclosure.

For this reason, lenders want a healthy cushion between your mortgage debt and your monthly income. They also want to see a reasonable cushion between your current total debt load (including credit cards, car loans, etc.) and your monthly income.

To determine if a mortgage payment is appropriate for your income, lenders will calculate what percentage of your gross monthly income it represents. Generally, the mortgage industry standard is that your monthly mortgage payment should not exceed about 28 percent of your gross monthly salary. For example, if your gross monthly salary is $4,000, your monthly payments should not be much higher than $1,120. Although 28 percent is not an absolute rule, if your payment represents a substantially higher percentage, you may be denied the mortgage you want.

As equally important and related measure of your capacity to repay the mortgage easily is your total debt load (including your proposed mortgage payment and any other debt payments) as a percentage of your monthly gross income. Lenders do not like to see this percentage rise over about 36 percent. This means that with monthly gross income of $4,000 and a proposed mortgage payment of $1,120, your other debt payments should not exceed $320 a month. Should your debt load be higher, you may need to reduce it before you qualify. A typical example of this is when a couple is making payments on two cars, creating a combined debt load (with the proposed mortgage payment) in excess of 36 percent. In this case the couple may need to sell one of their cars or to downsize vehicles to less expensive or used models to reduce their monthly debt payments to a qualifying level.

Occasionally, you can convince a lender to increase the debt-to-income ratio he or she will allow. This does not happen often, but is a possibility if you have a strong credit record and/or have already been paying housing costs higher than 28 percent for a substantial period of time. You may also be able to convince a lender to exceed the standard 28 percent if you can document an expected change in your financial circumstances, such as a raise or substantial reduction in consumer debt.

Poor Credit History

In addition to your total debt load, lenders are looking at your credit patterns to determine if you are a good risk. This will include reviewing your use of consumer debt such as credit cards and installment loans. If you have a pattern of frequent use of numerous credit cards and installment plans, with increasing balances that frequently approach your credit limits, lenders may be worried about your financial responsibility and deny your application even if you fit the percentage debt limits discussed above.

The best solution to this problem is to pay off as much debt as you can, consolidate the debt you have, close as many accounts as possible, and reduce your current use of these credit sources.

A history of frequent late charges, past-due accounts, and/or bankruptcy will be very damaging to your chances for mortgage approval. Lenders take a negligent attitude toward credit issues very seriously when they are assessing the risk you pose as a borrower. While lenders may make allowances for income and debt ratios, they are unlikely to make exceptions in their credit-history requirements.

If you have had a credit problem in the past due to unforeseen circumstances (e.g., layoff, high medical expenses), be forthcoming with your lender and explain the circumstances thoroughly. Isolated incidences may be overlooked. If, however, you have a history of late payments, overdue balances, and/or a bankruptcy without a reasonable explanation, you will need to start building a good credit record immediately.

Credit can often be repaired more quickly than you may be

led to believe by some lenders, especially those who are looking for an opportunity to charge you a higher rate due to a poor record. If there was ever a time to pull out of the market for a short time and get professional help, it is when there is a problem with your credit.

The first step you should take, however, is to determine that a problem actually exists. Throughout this book you have been urged to respond quickly to any credit problems you have. These rarely appear for the first time at the end of the process. If you are notified at the end of the process for the first time that there is a problem, you should immediately appeal your rejection. You are entitled to a copy of any report that is used to disqualify you. Is there an error in the report? Is there an explanation for any lapse in credit? Have you been given an opportunity to explain?

If there really is a problem, working with a nonprofit housing counseling agency in your community may put you back in the housing market in as little as six to twelve months. Like all other services, be sure you look into all the nonprofit counseling agencies in your area and select one that seems right for you.

Denial for Private Mortgage Insurance

This is the most unlikely situation, because the lender knows the standards before accepting your application. If your mortgage is declined because of the unavailability of mortgage insurance, appeal the decision and insist on an in-depth explanation for the denial.

Steps to Take if Your Application Is Rejected

If your loan application is rejected, you will need to know why so that you can take steps to get a mortgage elsewhere. Most important, however, is to remember that just because you are denied by one lender does not mean that you will necessarily be denied by another.

The lender is required to give you the reasons for rejection in writing. The form letter that you are likely to receive, however, is rarely enough information to explain specifically why you were rejected. Go back to your loan officer or, ideally, to the underwriter, and find out the specific reason your request was rejected. If you can explain the problem, your application may be reconsidered. Most mortgage rejections should come as no surprise. Throughout the mortgage-application process and while your paperwork is being completed, you should be notified about potential problems with your application.

Appealing Adverse Credit Decisions

If you believe your mortgage application was unfairly rejected, you should appeal the decision with the lender. In most cases, it is best to write a letter detailing the reasons why you believe the rejection decision should be reevaluated. Your tenacity also demonstrates to the lender your confidence in yourself and your repayment capacity.

Remember, do not be belligerent with a lender when appealing an adverse credit decision. Your best approach is to be deferential and to appear as reasonable and responsible as possible.

Before going out to look for another loan, and especially before taking a loan offer at a higher interest rate or less favorable terms (just to "get a loan now"), *stop* and consider your situation. Applying for and getting a more expensive loan that will cost you tens of thousands of dollars more may not be in your best interest.

A rejection may mean that it was not the right house for you or that it was not the right time for you to purchase a house. You may be better off finding another home or renting for a while as you repair your credit or build your income and savings.

Special Programs for Low- and Moderate-Income Households

Many low- and moderate-income households cannot qualify for mortgages under standard lending criteria. Many banks, however, participate in programs sponsored by government agencies and private organizations that are designed to make home ownership affordable for low- and moderate-income home buyers by providing financing with alternative lending guidelines.

To qualify for these programs, you will need to meet minimum- and maximum-income guidelines. You will also need to have a strong credit history. While most traditional lenders rely heavily on your past credit history when evaluating whether to give you a mortgage, the significance of a scant or no credit history may be diminished in some of these special lending programs. If your credit rating is bad, however, you may have a difficult time qualifying.

Typically, these low- and moderate-income home ownership programs are sponsored by the Department of Housing and Urban Development (HUD), Fannie Mae or Freddie Mac, state housing finance agencies, local housing departments, or non-profit housing groups. Check with your local lender for information on these programs or check your phone book's blue pages for government agency listings (usually found under "Housing").

CHAPTER 17

Discrimination in Mortgage Lending

Josephine is an Hispanic woman who contacted a mortgage lender about applying for a loan. In spite of the fact that the lender was in the business of making home loans, the person she spoke with did everything he could to dissuade her from applying for a home loan with the lender he represented.

Larry is a young black man who was making substantial improvements to his home in an up-and-coming inner-city neighborhood. He was surprised to learn, however that his home-improvement loan was approved in an amount significantly less than what he had anticipated. What's more, the interest rate was higher than the rate promised. It seems the appraised value on his home was not very high because of the neighborhood in which he lived.

Discrimination in mortgage lending may take several forms. It may be a direct negative reference to your race, national origin, religion, sex, age, source of income, or disability—the protected factors. Or it could be a direct negative reference to the predominant race or ethnicity of the neighborhood in which your future house is located. A direct negative reference is what is called a "smoking gun."

The most common form of discrimination in mortgage lending, however, occurs invisibly. It occurs when you are treated courteously by the loan originator, without any reference to your race, national origin, religion, sex, age, or disability. But you are discouraged from applying, referred elsewhere, offered less favorable costs or terms, or otherwise treated differently during processing because of these factors. If this occurs during the loan-application stage, it is not difficult to test for discrimination. If it occurs during processing, it is important for you to know how and where it may occur and how to respond.

You probably just want to buy a house and get a mortgage, not "test" for mortgage-lending discrimination. Since mortgage discrimination is widespread, however, you need to know how to spot it, how to avoid it, and what to do when you can't. Your goal as a home buyer is to get into the house you have selected. Many lending institutions do not discriminate; others do. Your best strategy is to find a non-discriminatory lender and get your mortgage. Then consider going back and taking action against any lenders who have discriminated against you.

There are three terms you need to understand: protected person or buyer, lender, and loan originator.

1. A *protected person* is one protected against discrimination in obtaining any loan (mortgage, second mortgage, or home-equity loan) secured by your dwelling by the Fair Housing Act and all forms of credit by the Equal Credit Opportunity Act. Under the Fair Housing law, persons are protected based on their race, color, religion, sex, national origin, familial status, and handicap. Under the Fair Lending or Equal Credit Opportunity law, persons are protected based on their race, color, religion, national origin, sex, marital status, age, receipt of income from public assistance, and the good-faith exercise of rights under the federal consumer-credit statutes.

2. A *lender* is any (a) bank, (b) savings and loan association, (c) mortgage company, or (d) credit union (if you are a member) that offers home mortgages, second mortgages, or home-equity loans. Mortgage or finance companies offering home loans may be independent companies or be owned by banks (bank-holding companies). There is no category that is necessarily better or worse when it comes to either discrimination or rate gouging. Since

there are good and bad actors in all categories, it is best to get information about different loan types available and rates from all types of lenders before selecting a mortgagor.

3. A *loan originator* is a generic term for the person who is selling you a mortgage—loan officers, loan counselors, mortgage brokers, and so forth. As a rule, loan originators are paid on commission based on the size of the mortgage and do not receive any pay unless they consummate your loan. Thus, they will not encourage you to apply if, based on their experience, they believe that your loan will not go through. Or if they see you as too much work (too many problems) for the amount of money they will make.

On the other hand, there are loan originators who may actively pursue your business because you are a woman, minority, or immigrant. They may assume you are under-educated in obtaining a mortgage or nervous about possible discrimination and will try to get away with selling you an above-market-rate mortgage. Doing so substantially increases the commission earned.

Knowing the laws that protect you will not help you avoid discrimination if you do not know the forms that discrimination takes. Therefore, this chapter will focus on these forms of discrimination and list sources for help (both counseling and legal), and where to file a complaint when you have evidence of discrimination. Even if you are not a protected person under the Civil Rights laws, this chapter will help you understand what lenders are looking for and how to submit a better application.

Avoiding Predators When Shopping for a Mortgage

Because discrimination meant less access to mortgages for minorities, immigrants, and women in the past, there are lenders who prey particularly on these people, suggesting that they will have a harder time in the regular marketplace. While these lenders say they will take good care of you, they often proffer interest rates and/or points far above the current market rates. The loan originators may themselves be minorities, immigrants, or women. They might be recommended by well-meaning but not well-educated friends, your realtor, or even your clergyman. More likely, though, they will knock on your door or have an office in your neighborhood. This is particularly true for refinancing. As a rule of thumb, if they knock on your door—do not do business with them.

Discrimination in mortgage lending is gradually subsiding, in good measure because of the increased attention to the subject and because the forms discrimination takes are now defined. As a result, lenders are held more accountable. There are, however, loan originators in your community and large companies for whom they work who have been charging minorities and immigrants, among others, far in excess of the going rate. They have no incentive to give up their more lucrative situation because the more they charge you above the market rate, the more money they make.

The U.S. Department of Justice is probing possible racial bias in loan pricing among home-mortgage lenders. The department has warned lenders that they are "free to price loans as they want, but they aren't permitted to base the price on someone's race."

Lenders often get away with overpricing because minorities, women, and immigrants get into a comfortable system of referrals, particularly with people similar in sex, race, or ethnicity, and don't check outside this comfortable system. When they do go out into the market to obtain a loan, they are easily discouraged. Often, minorities have no idea how hard it is for many people to get a mortgage, particularly at a good rate. However, opportunities abound.

If a number of seemingly insurmountable problems have been consistently identified by lenders that prevent you from getting the best rates in your market, it may be wise to postpone buying a house for six months to a year and work with a nonprofit housing-counseling agency or a local home buyers club in order to get a competitive-rate mortgage. If you must pay a premium interest rate because of your situation, the counselors will be able to refer you to a lender with the lowest interest rate for your situation.

Be sure you work with a nonprofit housing-counseling agency with Department of Housing and Urban Development (HUD)–certified counselors. This agency should not be affiliated with a lender. Often the same lenders known to gouge unsuspecting buyers offer "free" loan counseling—trying to sell you their product. Counseling services that employ HUD-certified counselors do not sell any loan products. Many of these organizations, however, have agreements with banks to accept "repaired" credit at market (not inflated) rates.

You can find a HUD-certified housing counselor by calling, toll free: 800-388-CCCS. You will be referred to the Consumer Credit Counseling Service in your area. There are two national organizations that also provide home ownership counseling throughout the United States. A call to the national office of ACORN (202) 547-2500 or the National Council of La Raza (202) 289-1380 will help you locate a counseling center in your area. In addition, your city or county housing and community development office probably funds housing counseling in your area and can give you referrals. Finally, check in the index of the yellow pages under "Housing assistance," or "Human" and/or "Social service" organizations.

Smoking Guns

While you are shopping, be alert for discrimination. The best time to shop for a mortgage is before or while you are shopping for a house, and the best way to find discrimination is to drop in, not call. Always "shop" with a pencil and paper in hand so that you can record whatever you hear. Make sure you know the name of the person you speak with. Get a business card before you begin your conversation. In addition to comparing costs, listen for signals of possible discrimination. These may be the smoking guns or, more likely, may be discouragement from applying at that institution.

Smoking guns at the application stage can be directed at random. References to neighborhood are commonplace, ranging from derogatory comments or questions about why you would want to live in that neighborhood (one that is predominantly African-American, ethnic, or racially/ethnically mixed) if you are white to derogatory comments about why you don't buy in "your own" neighborhoods if you are a protected class and you are buying in the suburbs or in a predominantly white neighborhood. Women-specific remarks might include: "How do you expect to take care of such a big house?" "Wouldn't a condominium be safer?" or "Shouldn't you be looking for a husband instead of a house?" Disabled persons may get similar comments.

If a loan originator suggests any of the above, try to get him/her to expand on the subject without putting words in his/her mouth. The best way is to repeat an unspecific part of what they said with a question mark. For example, the loan originator says, "You should be buying in your own neighborhood." Your response: "I should?" Do not be drawn into a discussion or argument. Do not repeat the negative things the loan originator says—only noncommittal questions. Carefully draw out the feelings of this person and record them while you are there if possible. Depart immediately after you have elicited from the loan originator as much as you can on the subject. Write a careful narrative (loan originator said, I said) of your entire visit just as soon as you leave the office. Don't wait until you return home, where you may be distracted. A well-recorded interview makes it possible to construct an appropriate "test" and improves your case. Also, be sure you have the person's card. Jot down a physical description, including age, size, race, hair color, and any other distinguishing features. Also, write down the time and date of the occurrence.

While you may not wish to file an application with that lender, you may have grounds to file a fair-housing complaint. If you do not have a contract in hand and choose to file a complaint, now is the time to do so. You may end up with a bargain-rate mortgage, no closing costs, and cash as part of your settlement, if successful. If you are under the gun for time with a contract in hand, proceed with another lender and consider filing a complaint later. If you have the time to pursue both the case and another mortgage, you may get your best settlement with a contract in hand.

Discouragement

Discrimination is more likely to occur in the first conversation when you request information, not after an application is filed. Whenever a protected applicant walks out of a lender's office without an application or without encouragement to apply, or having been told that you do not qualify, the protected applicant may have been treated differently from an unprotected applicant in similar financial circumstances.

Discouragement takes many forms. Sometimes it is outright refusal. "We don't make those kind of loans." "You wouldn't qualify for a fixed-rate loan." Sometimes it is in the form of "helpful" information such as: "We could do that loan, but as a first-time home buyer, you would do so much better with an FHA loan. We don't make FHA loans, but here is the name and number of a lender who does . . ." Sometimes it takes the form of a lack of engagement (i.e., the lender does not ask for financial information about you or your loan, will not tell you whether you qualify, or does not encourage you to apply).

Whatever the form discouragement takes, it is most often done with silk gloves. It can occur while you are graciously seated in the lender's office, offered coffee, a parking validation, and other courtesies. You may walk out thinking, "What nice people." But think again. You are offering them business (they make money by making loans). Yet they are discouraging you or sending you to another lender for a better buy. Would a Buick dealer send you to a Chevy dealer because Chevys are a better buy than Buicks? The dealer would move heaven and earth to persuade you to buy that Buick.

Rest assured, most lenders bend over backward to offer prospects they want to do business with helpful information and to give them "tricks of the trade." They tell them about gift letters, about applying on payday when you have the most money in the bank, about closing the end of the month to reduce closing costs, about how to pay off or rearrange debt so you look better, about how to get letters to explain any credit discrepancies, and about exceptions to the rules.

Self-testing for Discrimination

Finding discrimination is easiest before a lending decision is made. In fact, the less said, the easier it is to "test" for discrimination. For example, Maria Torres goes into a lender and asks for information about a mortgage. She indicates she can afford a 10 percent down payment. The lender tells her they only do mortgages with 20 percent down payments. Maria gets the lender's card, leaves the office, and immediately writes down what she said and what the lender said. Maria tells her white, non-Hispanic friend at work about her experience and asks for her help as a "tester." Mary Jones goes to the same lender and asks for information about a mortgage. She volunteers that she has enough cash only for a 10 percent down payment. She is told that while they normally require a 20 percent down payment, there is, however, an exception for which she might qualify that would allow them to make a loan to her with only 10 percent down.

This is a hypothetical case, but one that a jury can understand. If Maria had submitted an application and the lender had rejected it for cause, the lender could bring in all kinds of experts to explain why Maria's application was a poor risk. On the other hand, without any specific financial data and credit information, the lender has no defense for telling one applicant about exceptions and not the other, particularly since one applicant is Hispanic and the other is not.

When and how do you test? For protected persons applying for a mortgage, the first rule is: never accept no as a given. If you are told no, or are discouraged from applying for a mortgage for any reason, suspect discrimination and "test" it.

Find a white (or a male) friend or colleague to test for you. Do not tell your tester what the loan originator said to you—tell him only what you said. The tester should write this down and offer only as much information as you did. The tester should concentrate on the loan originator's response and record the conversation immediately afterward. If the loan originator encouraged your tester to apply, or gave him different information that would make him eligible while you were told you were ineligible, you may wish to file a complaint.

Selecting a Lender to File an Application

The ideal is to find a lending institution with competitive rates, a loan originator who makes you confident that you will be well taken care of, and a lender that wants your business. Equally important is to review the lender's rejection and withdrawal rates for African-American and Hispanic applicants. This is published each year by the Federal Reserve, as required by the Home Mortgage Disclosure Act (HMDA), and is deposited in a "central depository" in each metropolitan area. Call the Federal Financial Institutions Examination Council (FFIEC) at 202-634-6526 to find out where this information is available in your community. While all lenders must also make this information available upon request, this information is often difficult to obtain from individual lenders.

Another source is your local newspaper. Many newspapers have found that this makes a good story and will publish the results each year. While they are not likely to publish all lenders, they are likely to publish the ones with the highest rejection rates (those to avoid) and the lowest rejection rates (those to patronize). They are not likely, however, to publish the "withdrawn" rates. So if you go to the central depository, take note of high minority withdrawal rates. Then avoid lenders with high withdrawal rates. These are usually cases where the lender drags the application beyond a reasonable period without a commitment and borrowers withdraw them.

Avoiding Discrimination in the Application Process

If you've done your shopping well, you will have a good idea of your strengths and weaknesses. If you specifically meet the lender's standards (i.e., have perfect credit, a sufficient down payment, two or more years on the same job, and adequate income), you are less likely to be turned down based on discrimination.

If you have any weaknesses (e.g., some late payments on your credit report or frequent job changes but steady income), discuss those up-front with your loan originator before you apply. Develop a plan with your loan originator's assistance as to how those weaknesses will be addressed. At a minimum, with your application submit a carefully constructed letter about each identified weakness.

Once you have filed an application, discrimination is likely to occur if you: (1) need an exception to the lender's rule, (2) are self-employed, underemployed (short-term or part-time), or rely on tips or overtime pay to qualify, (3) are employed in blue-collar, labor, or menial-job categories, or (4) have any credit problems.

Obtaining an exception to the lender's rule is the most likely place to find discrimination once an application has been filed. It is often called the "thin file" syndrome. When a discrimination complaint is filed and investigators go into the files, minorities generally have thinner files. Most often it occurs because they are not offered the opportunity to explain their exceptions to the rule. This is why it is so important to take the initiative to explain your situation and thicken your file when you submit your application. If you wait for the lender to ask you to explain your position, the chances are greater that you not only won't be asked, but that you will be rejected.

Bias against self-employed persons also exists, regardless of whether or not they are minorities. For self-employed women and minorities, however, obtaining a mortgage may be extremely difficult.

The following recommendations are offered. First, if you currently have a job and are considering self-employment, if possible stay in your job until you buy your house. The same thing is true with changing jobs. If you currently have a job and can remain there, stay in place until you close on your mortgage. Second, if you are currently self-employed and want to buy a house, start planning at least two years in advance. It will be difficult to obtain credit in excess of the amount justified by the two previous years (as reflected on your federal tax returns), even if your business has improved one hundred percent in the last six months. Business owners who show a good income over a long period of time on their IRS form 1040 are generally considered good risks among the self-employed. If you are a business owner who does not show a good income over a long period of time, plan on lots of supporting documentation and plan on shopping around. A 20 percent or higher down payment will also probably help.

Moving from job to job, having several jobs, or having untraditional employment is also a problem, particularly if you are in the protected group. In such cases you need to show continuity of employment. In addition to your IRS form 1040 for the last several years, submit letters from current employers who say how good your work is and from past employers who say not only how good your work was, but how they hated to let you go! If possible, have the letters stress that you are an excellent worker and that your skills are very much in demand. Nonprofit housing counseling agencies can be very helpful with preparing this documentation and suggesting lenders. Again, particularly if you are a minority or other protected person, do your own shopping as well before you file an application for a loan.

In computing what you can afford to pay for housing, the lender should include all of your income, including that of your entire family that lives with you. You must, however, be prepared to prove that they live with you and that you or they reported that income on an IRS form 1040. If you are self- or underemployed and/or have many different sources of income, working with a nonprofit housing counseling agency would be very helpful for you in putting this information together.

Some lenders also have a bias against those employed in blue-collar, laborer, or menial categories of work. They often define this source of income as a greater risk and try to charge a higher rate. In many cases it is a cover for racial or ethnic discrimination.

If you meet all the lender's criteria, it may not matter how you make your living. This bias is more likely to appear when you need an exception to the lender's criteria or if the loan originator thinks he or she can get away with charging a higher rate of interest. If, for example, you've worked for only six months in your present job, get rave letters from your former and present employers saying how valuable you are. If you regularly work overtime, document it carefully and get a letter saying that it can be expected to continue forever.

Many people have perfect credit. However, if lenders gave mortgages only to those who have perfect credit, the mortgage industry would be half its present size. Among those with less than perfect credit, there is an occasional blip caused by a job loss, illness, or even a disagreement between you and a merchant. Most often these can be explained. As discussed above, however, protected persons face the thin-file syndrome. This is particularly the case with credit. Exceptions in credit standards that are made for unprotected persons are often not made for protected persons.

If your credit history is scant or has blemishes, don't wait to be asked for an explanation. Make certain to submit a letter of explanation with your application!

Warning Signs in the Application Process

Needless to say, a smoking gun is a definite sign of discrimination. It is very unlikely that you will receive anything in writing from the lender that is blatantly discriminatory. You never know, however, when a loan originator has an imprudent moment and shares something that is either discriminatory or reveals discrimination in the inner workings of the lender.

Once you have filed your application, there are warning signs of trouble. These are not necessarily discrimination, but to suspect discrimination is prudent. These warning signs include: (1) failure to give you a conditional commitment within the time limit they set for themselves (sometimes as little as twenty-four hours or as long as two weeks); (2) denial of the loan at the last minute based on something that they knew at the beginning; (3) denial of the loan based on the appraised value of the property; and (4) denial of the loan based on inability to obtain private mortgage insurance (PMI).

If the lender accepts your application and filing fee but does not tell you within two weeks that you will be approved, subject only to verification of the data you have given them, you might suspect the possibility of discrimination. By this time all problems should be on the table and discussed, and most verifications should be in. Some lenders hold minority applications and neither approve nor deny them until, in frustration, the applicants withdraw the application because of inaction. After waiting two weeks, insist on a written commitment, subject to final verification of facts.

As a caveat, do not confuse commitment with verification. Verification can be seemingly endless, picayune, and random (a new call every day for some other piece of information). This is the nature of the beast, not necessarily discrimination. In fact, if your lender is calling you often, you know your loan is being processed. If they don't call you frequently for more verification, contact them and find out what's going on.

If the lender denies your loan at the last minute, or tries to raise the interest rate, based on something they knew at the beginning, discrimination may be occurring. Examples include: you are denied for insufficient job experience, yet on your application you stated that you had your job for only six months; or you are denied for insufficient income, yet your income is based on overtime, and you stated that on a letter from your employer that you submitted with your application; or you are denied for poor credit, yet the lender had your credit report and your explanation within twenty-four hours after you filed your application.

If the lender denies your application, the denial and cause for denial must be submitted to you in writing. Regardless of cause stated, but particularly if "insufficient collateral" is stated, ask for a copy of your appraisal. A low appraisal will reduce the value of your collateral and therefore lower the amount you can borrow. It is wise to obtain the appraisal because sometimes a lender will have a low appraisal but will state another reason for denial rather than draw attention to the appraisal.

If your mortgage is for a house in a minority neighborhood, a central city neighborhood, or a changing or racially mixed neighborhood and it is denied for any reason, unreasonably delayed, or you have even the slightest suspicion of discrimination, request your appraisal and get it into the hands of an expert in lending discrimination. There is no better place to find a smoking gun than in an appraisal.

Regulation B, implementing the Equal Credit Opportunity Act, requires creditors to provide applicants, within thirty days, with a copy of appraisal reports for credit secured by a residential structure. Some lenders will automatically give you a copy of your appraisal. All lenders, however, are required by law to inform you in writing that "you have the right to a copy of the appraisal report used in connection with your application for credit." This disclosure further states that you must request the copy of the appraisal, in writing, within ninety days of a credit decision, or within ninety days of withdrawing your application.

If your application is denied because of unavailability of private mortgage insurance (PMI), go directly to the head of the mortgage-lending division in your area and find out the name of the private mortgage insurer who denied your insurance.

Ask how they chose that insurer, ask to see the insurer's printed standards, and ask for the rejection form or letter. Ask if they tried any other insurers, and if so, whom did they try, and state that you would like to see their standards and rejection letters also. Ask to see their standard book to see if there are any insurers whose standards you meet. Hopefully, this will get you your PMI, and you will be able to go to closing.

PMIs publish their standards up-front, and every lender has a book of each PMI and their standards. Therefore, every lender knows at the time they accept your application, and certainly by the time they give you your commitment, whether or not you meet the standards for one or more of several private mortgage insurers. (The number of PMIs serving your lender is related to the size of the city or the size of the lender. Large cities and large lenders have dozens of insurers from which to choose.)

Where to File a Complaint

There are more choices and opportunities every year. As a starter, if you qualify as a protected person under the Fair Housing Act, you may file a complaint with the Department of Housing and Urban Development (HUD). HUD's toll-free number for fair housing complaints is: 800-669-9777. You will be referred to an office near you. However, do not expect quick action from HUD.

The Fair Housing Act is one of the few laws that allows access to the courts without first attempting administrative remedy. It also affords you the option of doing both. Finally, it provides for punitive damages so that going to court can be far more satisfying. Therefore, you should probably start with a lawyer. Then, if action is warranted, file appropriate administrative complaints. You can go into court when and if your attorney feels the time is right.

It is important to file a complaint with HUD as well as with your local and state human rights commission. Filing with everyone you can is important because your complaint may not be the only one against a particular lender. In fact, your case will be considerably strengthened if yours is not the first complaint against this lender. Also, HUD and local or state agencies will research your case. If you're not happy with their proposed conciliation, you can still take the lender to court.

Carefully selecting a lawyer is as important as carefully selecting a lender. Ideally you want one with experience, if not with lending discrimination, at least with the Fair Housing Act. Also, you want one who will be willing to take a fee at settlement, except for out-of-pocket costs. Talk with everyone who is available before making a decision. Ask specifically about a lawyer's experience and success in Fair Housing and Fair Lending.

Resources for legal assistance include:

1. The John Marshall Law School Fair Housing Legal Support Center in Chicago, Illinois, which provides ongoing training to lawyers in fair housing and maintains a national registry of lawyers with experience and/or training in the field. In addition, a new legal research database system for fair housing is now available to all attorneys to assist them in serving you better. Their phone number is 312-987-2397.
2. The Lawyer's Committee for Civil Rights has offices in a number of major cities, and they do excellent legal work in fair housing. Their national office is in Washington, D.C., and the phone number is: 202-662-8600.
3. The "Fair Housing" or "Civil Rights" association(s) in your area generally work with area lawyers on fair-housing cases. If you can't find them through directory assistance, they may be members of the National Fair Housing Alliance in Washington, D.C. The National Alliance's phone number is 202-898-1661.
4. ACORN Fair Housing is located in many cities and may have good legal referrals. Their national office is in Washington, D.C., and the phone number is: 202-547-2500.

5. Local chapters of the NAACP, Urban League, and National Council of La Raza often do work in fair housing as well as housing counseling. Check with them for referrals or to see if they have lawyers on staff.
6. Many law schools have housing clinics, but you will want to make sure that they have experience or training specifically in "fair housing" as compared with general "housing" law.
7. Many state and local human rights commissions can refer you to a private lawyer as well. They are listed in the yellow pages under state, county, and/or city government.

Filing under the Fair Housing Act rather than the ECOA is preferred for both easy access to the courts and for obtaining actual and punitive damages. If you are not a protected person under the Fair Housing Act but are only protected under ECOA, or if you have been refused access to your appraisal, you should file a complaint under the Equal Credit Opportunity Act. File a complaint with the federal regulator with jurisdiction over the particular lender. See the Appendix for a listing of these agencies.

Finally, a few states have strong civil rights protections in their banking laws. Check under state governments for the banking regulatory agency in your state and call to see what additional protections they might provide against discrimination and if they take complaints. They might just be looking into your lender's practices at the time you find probable evidence of discrimination.

CHAPTER 18

Resolving Mortgage Complaints

*Butch and Sherry wanted to buy a new home but ran into prob-
lems with a mortgage lender who didn't adequately disclose some
of the costs relating to their mortgage. As a result, although they
had spent endless hours providing documentation for this particular lender, they backed down and refused to close on the
house.*

The preceding chapter identified several different ways to complain about discriminatory practices by lenders. This chapter
identifies how you should pursue complaints unrelated to
discrimination.

You are entitled to access to information, specific legal
rights, and protection against certain abusive practices under
federal consumer-lending statutes and possibly state consumer-
protection statutes. These cover a variety of consumer rights.
For example, you are protected if your lender significantly mis-
represents the cost of the mortgage, deliberately drags his feet
so you miss your interest-rate lock-in date, or fails to provide
you with a fee disclosure before your closing date.

If you feel that you have been subjected to an improper practice, you should contact one or more of the following organizations to determine if your rights have been violated:

- The federal regulator with jurisdiction over your lender
  (you may find this agency by referring to the information

contained later in this chapter, by asking the lender, or by contacting your state attorney general's office)

- Local nonprofit housing agencies
- Legal assistance programs
- Local nonprofit or governmental consumer organizations

If you determine that you have grounds for complaint and you wish to pursue enforcement of your rights, your options are listed below.

How and Where to Complain

First Complain to Your Mortgage Lender

You should first complain directly to the mortgage lender or broker against which you have a complaint. Go directly to the unit involved. Speak to the manager of the person against whom you have the complaint. In verbal communications with financial-provider employees, speak calmly but firmly. Above all, be persistent. Do not let them pass the buck or ignore you. If you are not satisfied with responses, jot down names, titles, and telephone numbers.

If this does not speedily resolve your problem, do not rely on the decisions of subordinates. Go immediately to the top. Find out the name and address of an officer or the person in charge and send your complaint to that person. If it is a large organization, appeal to the head of the department, the divisional manager, or the president of the company.

At this point, put your complaint in writing. In your letter, make sure to present your version of the situation and why you feel a complaint is necessary. Identify both your problem and the remedy you seek. If you believe a federal law or regulation has been violated, make it clear that you are aware of the law. Give the lender your preferred resolution of the problem as well as a prioritized listing of options that might also resolve the conflict. Ask for a prompt response by a certain date (for example, within two weeks). Indicate in your letter that you are attempting to resolve the matter directly with the lender. However, you will be left with no other alternative but to complain to their regulator if they fail to make a good-faith effort to work with you toward resolution. If the officer you contact fails to reply by the deadline you have set, send a follow-up letter, call to check on the status of your complaint, or file a complaint with the appropriate federal regulatory agency. Keep copies of all correspondence for your files and possible further use.

In many cases your complaint will be referred by higher-ups back to the first unit you contacted. But this time it will probably get the attention it deserves. If things are not resolved to your satisfaction after the second go-around, call the bank officer again to let him or her know you still have a problem.

Complain to the Appropriate Federal Regulatory Agency

Before complaining about your lender to a federal regulatory agency, you first need to determine which federal regulatory agency has jurisdiction. Ask your lender for the name, address, and telephone number of this agency. You can also determine the appropriate federal regulatory agency from the information provided below. The national offices are listed below. For a listing of regional offices around the country, consult the Appendix.

Nationally chartered banks ("National" or "NA" appears in the name):

Comptroller of the Currency
Consumer Activities Division
250 E Street, S.W.
Washington, DC 20219

State-chartered banks (FDIC-insured and a member of the Federal Reserve System):

Federal Reserve Board
Division of Consumer & Community Affairs
20th & Constitution Avenues, N.W.
Washington, DC 20551

State-chartered banks (FDIC-insured but not a member of the Federal Reserve System):

Federal Deposit Insurance Corporation
Office of Consumer Affairs
550 17th Street, N.W.
Washington, DC 20429

Federally chartered or insured savings and loan association:

Office of Thrift Supervision
Consumer Affairs
1700 G Street, N.W.
Washington, DC 20552

Federally chartered credit union ("Federal Credit Union" appears in the name):

National Credit Union Administration
1776 G Street, N.W.
Washington, DC 20456

State-chartered credit union, mortgage company, finance company, government lending program, state-chartered banks, or savings institutions without FDIC insurance:

Federal Trade Commission
Bureau of Consumer Protection
Office of Credit Practices
Sixth & Pennsylvania, N.W.
Washington, DC 20580

Direct your letter of complaint to the appropriate agency. You might consider mailing a copy of the letter you send to the federal regulatory agency to the institution against which you are lodging the complaint. If the institution knows you are taking your complaint to a higher authority, it may be more willing to accommodate your request.

A complaint to a federal regulatory agency must be in writing. When filing a complaint, give as much information as possible containing your side of the story, including specific details (dates and times, your activities, company responses, names of persons with whom you have spoken, etc.). Send along copies of any relevant materials (letters you have sent or received, copies of account or loan documents, etc.).

Since federal regulatory agencies are not responsible for resolving individual cases, do not expect them to intercede on your behalf once they receive your complaint. Your complaint will be grouped with other consumer complaints and investigated. Your complaint, along with others, may alert the agency to a violation of a federal consumer statute. These complaints might help the agency determine if a pattern of practice exists (for example, a particular institution has been violating the law with respect to other people as well). Armed with the information you provide, examiners will scrutinize an institution in the area of your complaint on their next visit.

Contact Local News Media and Consumer Organizations

If you think your gripe with a particular lender is something other borrowers are being subjected to, contact local news media representatives to see if they might be enticed to a story on the problem. Negative publicity is something most institutions will try to avoid at all costs. In addition, if the problem is fairly widespread, contact local consumer organizations that handle consumer complaints to see if they will get involved. To have a local advocacy group interceding on your behalf or squawking publicly about your problem would add fuel to the fire and might prompt the institution to respond favorably.

Sue in Federal Court

If you wish to pursue legal action, consult with an attorney about bringing a suit in federal court against your financial-services provider. You can usually either bring a suit in your own right or participate in a class-action suit. While it may not be worth your while to pursue legal action over a five dollar dispute, a class-action suit (where you are joined by other people who have been subjected to the same practice) may be more appropriate.

Pursue State and Local Actions

You may also be protected under a state law, since some states have enacted laws to protect their citizens concerning certain consumer financial transactions. Consult with a local attorney to see if your state has enacted such a law. If so, you should be able to file a complaint with the appropriate state agency (such as the state banking commission, state and local consumer-protection agencies, state attorney general's office). You might also try contacting the local Better Business Bureau. In addition, you may be able to sue in a state court. Again, check with a local attorney to see whether this is possible.

Appendix:
Federal Regulatory Agency Addresses

Department of Housing and Urban Development
451 Seventh Street, S.W.
Washington, DC 20410

REGIONAL OFFICES

New England
HUD Massachusetts State
  Office
Thomas P. O'Neill, Jr.,
  Federal Building
10 Causeway Street
Boston, MA 02222-1092

New York/New Jersey
HUD New York State Office
26 Federal Plaza
New York, NY 10278-0068

Mid-Atlantic
HUD Pennsylvania State Office
The Wanamaker Building
100 Penn Square East
Philadelphia, PA 19107-3390

Southeast/Caribbean
HUD Georgia State Office
Richard B. Russell Federal
  Building
75 Spring Street, S.W.
Atlanta, GA 30303-3388

Midwest
HUD Illinois State Office
Ralph Metcalfe Federal
  Building
77 West Jackson Boulevard
Chicago, IL 60604-3507

Southwest
HUD Texas State Office
1600 Throckmorton
P.O. Box 2905
Fort Worth, TX 76113-2905

Great Plains
HUD Kansas State Office
Gateway Tower II
400 State Avenue
Kansas City, KS 66101-2406

Rocky Mountains
HUD Colorado State Office
633 Seventeenth Street
Denver, CO 80202-3607

Pacific/Hawaii
HUD California State Office
Philip Burton Federal
   Building & U.S. Courthouse
450 Golden Gate Avenue
P.O. Box 36003
San Francisco, CA 94102-3448

Northwest/Alaska
HUD Washington State
   Office
Suite 200, Seattle
   Federal Office Building
909 First Avenue
Seattle, WA 98104-1000

Comptroller of the Currency
250 E Street, S.W.
Washington, DC 20219

DISTRICT OFFICES

Northeastern
1114 Avenue of the Americas
Suite 3900
New York, NY 10036-7780

Southeastern
Marquis One Tower
Suite 600
245 Peachtree Center
   Avenue, N.E.
Atlanta, GA 30303-1223

Western
50 Fremont Street
Suite 3900
San Francisco, CA 94105-2292

Central
One Financial Plaza
Suite 2700
440 South LaSalle Street
Chicago, IL 60605-1073

Midwestern
2345 Grand Avenue
Suite 700
Kansas City, MO 64108-2683

Southwestern
1600 Lincoln Plaza
500 North Akard Street
Dallas, TX 75201-3394

Federal Reserve System
Twentieth Street and Constitution Avenue, N.W.
Washington, DC 20551

REGIONAL OFFICES

Boston
600 Atlantic Avenue
Boston, MA 02106

New York
33 Liberty Street
Federal Reserve P.O. Station
New York, NY 10045

Philadelphia
Ten Independence Mall
Philadelphia, PA 19106

Cleveland
1455 East Sixth Street
Cleveland, OH 44114

Richmond
701 East Byrd Street
Richmond, VA 23219

Atlanta
104 Marietta Street, N.W.
Atlanta, GA 30303-2713

Chicago
230 South LaSalle Street
Chicago, IL 60604

St. Louis
411 Locust Street
St. Louis, MO 63102

Minneapolis
250 Marquette Avenue
Minneapolis, MN 55401-2171

Kansas City
925 Grand Boulevard
Kansas City, MO 64198

Dallas
2200 North Pearl Street
Dallas, TX 75222

San Francisco
101 Market Street
San Francisco, CA 90015

National Credit Union Administration
1775 Duke Street
Alexandria, VA 22314-3428

REGIONAL OFFICES

Region I
9 Washington Square
Albany, NY 12205

Region II
1775 Duke Street
Alexandria, VA 22314-3437

Region III
7000 Central Parkway
Atlanta, GA 30328

Region IV
4225 Naperville Road
Lisle, IL 60532

Region V
4807 Spicewood Springs Road
Austin, TX 78759-8490

Region VI
2300 Clayton Road
Concord, CA 94520

Federal Trade Commission
Sixth Street & Pennsylvania Avenue, N.W.
Washington, DC 20580

REGIONAL OFFICES

Atlanta
1718 Peachtree Street, N.W.
Room 1000
Atlanta, GA 30367

Boston
101 Merrimac Street
Suite 810
Boston, MA 02114-4719

Chicago
55 East Monroe Street
Suite 1860
Chicago, IL 60603

Cleveland
668 Euclid Avenue
Suite 520-A
Cleveland, OH 44114

Dallas
100 N. Central Expressway
Suite 500
Dallas, TX 75201

Denver
1961 Stout Street
Suite 1523
Denver, CO 80294

Los Angeles
11000 Wilshire Boulevard
Suite 13209
Los Angeles, CA 90024

New York
150 William Street
Suite 1300
New York, NY 10038

San Francisco
901 Market Street
Suite 570
San Francisco, CA 94103

Seattle
2806 Federal Building
915 Second Avenue
Seattle, WA 98174

**Office of Thrift Supervision
Department of the Treasury
1700 G Street, N.W.
Washington, DC 20552**

REGIONAL OFFICES

New Jersey
10 Exchange Place Centre
18th Floor
Jersey City, NJ 07302

Atlanta
1475 Peachtree Street, N.E.
Atlanta, GA 30309

Chicago
111 East Wacker Drive
Suite 800
Chicago, IL 60601-4360

Dallas
122 W. John Carpenter
   Freeway
Suite 600
Irving, TX 75039-2010

San Francisco
1 Montgomery Street
Suite 400
San Francisco, CA 94104

A Consumer's Glossary of Mortgage Terms

Acceleration clause: allows the lender to speed up the rate at which your loan comes due or even to demand immediate payment of the entire outstanding balance of the loan should you default on your loan.

Adjustable rate mortgage (ARM): a mortgage in which the interest rate is adjusted periodically based on a preselected index. Also sometimes known as the renegotiable-rate mortgage, the variable-rate mortgage, or the Canadian-rollover mortgage.

Adjustment interval: on an adjustable-rate mortgage, the time between changes in the interest rate and/or monthly payment, typically one, three, or five years, depending on the index.

Amortization: loan payment by equal periodic payments calculated to pay off the debt at the end of a fixed period, including accrued interest on the outstanding balance.

Annual percentage rate (APR): an interest rate reflecting the cost of a mortgage as a yearly rate. This rate is likely to be higher than the stated note rate or advertised rate on the mortgage, because it takes into account points and other credit costs. The APR allows home buyers to compare different types of mortgages based on the annual cost for each loan.

Source: Mortgage Bankers Association of America

Appraisal: an estimate of the value of property, made by a qualified professional called an appraiser.

Assumption: an agreement between buyer and seller in which the buyer takes over the payments on an existing mortgage from the seller. Assuming a loan can usually save the buyer money, since this is an existing mortgage debt, unlike a new mortgage, where closing costs and new, possibly higher, market-rate interest charges will apply.

Balloon (payment) mortgage: usually a short-term fixed-rate loan that involves small payments for a certain period of time and one large payment for the remaining amount of the principal at a time specified in the contract.

Broker: an individual in the business of assisting in arranging funding or negotiating contracts for a client but who does not loan the money himself. Brokers usually charge a fee or receive a commission for their services.

Buy-down: when a lender and/or a home builder subsidizes the mortgage by lowering the interest rate during the first few years of the loan. While the payments are initially low, they will increase when the subsidy expires.

Caps (interest): consumer safeguards that limit the amount the interest rate on an adjustable-rate mortgage may change per year and/or the life of the loan.

Caps (payment): consumer safeguards that limit the amount monthly payments on an adjustable-rate mortgage may change.

Closing: a meeting between a buyer, seller, and lender or their agents when the property and funds legally change hands. Also called settlement.

Closing costs: usually include an origination fee, discount points, appraisal fee, title search and insurance, survey, taxes, deed-recording fee, credit-report charge, and other costs assessed at settlement. The costs of closing usually are about three to six percent of the mortgage amount.

Commitment: an agreement, often in writing, between a lender and a borrower to loan money at a future date subject to the completion of paperwork or compliance with stated conditions.

Construction loan: a short-term interim loan for financing the cost of construction. The lender advances funds to the builder at periodic intervals as the work progresses.

Conventional loan: a mortgage not insured by FHA or guaranteed by the VA or Farmers Home Administration (FmHA).

Credit report: a report documenting the credit history and current status of a borrower's credit standing.

Debt-to-income ratio: a ratio, expressed as a percentage, that results when a borrower's monthly payment obligation on long-term debts is divided by his or her net effective income (FHA/VA loans) or gross monthly income (conventional loans). See *housing expenses-to-income ratio.*

Deed of trust: in many states, this document is used in place of a mortgage to secure the payment of a note.

Default: failure to meet legal obligations in a contract, specifically, failure to make the monthly payments on a mortgage.

Deferred interest: see *negative amortization.*

Delinquency: failure to make payments on time. This can lead to foreclosure.

Department of Veterans Affairs (VA): an independent agency of the federal government that guarantees long-term, low- or no-down-payment mortgages to eligible veterans.

Discount point: see *points.*

Down payment: money paid to make up the difference between the purchase price and the mortgage amount. Down payments usually are ten to twenty percent of the sales price on conventional loans, and no money down up to five percent on FHA and VA loans.

Due-on-sale-clause: a provision in a mortgage or deed of trust that allows the lender to demand immediate payment of the balance of the mortgage if the mortgage holder sells the home.

Earnest money: money given by a buyer to a seller as part of the purchase price to bind a transaction or assure payment.

Equal Credit Opportunity Act (ECOA): a federal law that requires lenders and other creditors to make credit equally available without discrimination based on race, color, religion, national origin, age, sex, marital status, or receipt of income from public assistance programs.

Equity: the difference between the fair market value and current indebtedness, also referred to as the owner's interest.

Escrow: a neutral third party who carries out the instructions of both the buyer and seller to handle all the paperwork settlement or "closing." Escrow may also refer to an account held by the lender into which the home buyer pays money for tax or insurance payments.

Fannie Mae: see *Federal National Mortgage Association.*

Farmers Home Administration (FmHA): provides financing to farmers and other qualified borrowers who are unable to obtain loans elsewhere.

Federal Home Loan Bank Board (FHLBB): a regulatory and supervisory agency for federally chartered savings institutions.

Federal Home Loan Mortgage Corporation (FHLMC): Also called "Freddie Mac." A quasi-governmental agency that purchases conventional mortgages from insured depository institutions and HUD-approved mortgage bankers.

Federal Housing Administration (FHA): a division of the Department of Housing and Urban Development. Its main activity is the insuring of residential mortgage loans made by private lenders. FHA also sets standards for underwriting mortgages.

Federal National Mortgage Association (FNMA): Also known as "Fannie Mae." A tax-paying corporation created by Congress that purchases and sells conventional residential mortgages as well as those insured by FHA or guaranteed by VA. This institution, which provides funds for one in seven mortgages, makes mortgage money more available and more affordable.

FHA loan: a loan insured by the Federal Housing Administration open to all qualified home purchasers. While there are limits to the size of FHA loans ($124,875), they are generous enough to handle moderately-priced homes almost anywhere in the country.

FHA mortgage insurance: requires a small fee (up to 3.8 percent of the loan amount) paid at closing or a portion of this fee added to each monthly payment of an FHA loan to insure the loan with FHA. On a 9.5 percent $75,000, thirty-year fixed-rate FHA loan, this fee would amount to either $2,850 at closing or an extra $31 a month for the life of the loan. In addition, FHA mortgage insurance requires an annual fee of 0.5 percent of the current loan amount, paid in monthly installments. The lower the down payment, the more years the fee must be paid.

Fixed-rate mortgage: a mortgage on which the interest rate is set for the term of the loan.

Foreclosure: a legal procedure in which property securing debt is sold by the lender to pay the defaulting borrower's debt.

Freddie Mac: see *Federal Home Loan Mortgage Corporation.*

Ginnie Mae: see *Government National Mortgage Association.*

Government National Mortgage Association (GNMA): Also known as "Ginnie Mae." Provides sources of funds for residential mortgages, insured or guaranteed by FHA or VA.

Graduated-payment mortgage (GPM): a type of flexible-payment mortgage in which the payments increase for a specified period of time and then level off. This type of mortgage has negative amortization built into it.

Gross monthly income: the total amount the borrower earns per month, before any expenses are deducted.

Guaranty: a promise by one party to pay a debt or perform an obligation contracted by another if the original party fails to pay or perform according to a contract.

Hazard insurance: a form of insurance in which the insurance company protects the insured from specified losses, such as fire, windstorm, and the like.

Housing expenses-to-income ratio: the ratio, expressed as a percentage, that results when a borrower's housing expenses are divided by his or her net effective income (FHA/VA loans) or gross monthly income (conventional loans). See *debt-to-income ratio.*

Impound: that portion of a borrower's monthly payments held by the lender or servicer to pay for taxes, hazard insurance, mortgage insurance, lease payments, and other items as they become due. Also known as *reserves.*

Index: a published interest rate against which lenders measure the difference between the current interest rate on an adjustable-rate mortgage and that earned by other investments (such as one-, three-, and five-year U.S. Treasury security yields, the monthly average interest rate on loans closed by savings and loan institutions, and the monthly average costs of funds incurred by savings and loans), which is then used to adjust the interest rate on an adjustable mortgage up or down.

Investor: a money source for a lender.

Jumbo loan: a loan that is larger (more than $191,250) than the limits set by the Federal National Mortgage Association and the Federal Home Loan Mortgage Corporation. Because jumbo loans cannot be funded by these two agencies, they usually carry a higher interest rate.

Lien: a claim on a piece of property for the payment or satisfaction of a debt or obligation.

Loan-to-value ratio: the relationship between the amount of a mortgage loan and the appraised value of the property expressed as a percentage.

Margin: the amount a lender adds to the index on an adjustable-rate mortgage to establish the adjusted interest rate.

Market value: the highest price that a buyer would pay and the lowest price a seller would accept on a property. Market value may be different from the price a property could actually be sold for at a given time.

Mortgage insurance: money paid to insure the mortgage when the down payment is less than twenty percent. See *private mortgage insurance, FHA mortgage insurance.*

Mortgagee: the lender.

Mortgagor: the borrower or homeowner.

Negative amortization: this occurs when your monthly payments are not large enough to pay all the interest due on a loan. This unpaid interest is added to the unpaid balance of the loan. The danger of negative amortization is that the home buyer ends up owing more than the original amount of the loan.

Net effective income: the borrower's gross income minus federal income tax.

Nonassumption clause: a statement in a mortgage contract forbidding the assumption of the mortgage without the prior approval of the lender.

Origination fee: a fee charged by a lender to prepare loan documents, make credit checks, inspect and sometimes appraise a property; usually computed as a percentage of the face value of the loan.

PITI: principal, interest, taxes, and insurance. Also called monthly housing expense.

Points (loan discount points): prepaid interest assessed at closing by the lender. Each point is equal to one percent of the loan amount (e.g., two points on a $100,000 mortgage would cost $2,000).

Power of attorney: a legal document authorizing one person to act on behalf of another.

Prepaids: expenses necessary to create an escrow account or to adjust the seller's existing escrow account. Can include taxes, hazard insurance, private mortgage insurance, and special assessments.

Prepayment penalty: money charged for an early repayment of debt. Prepayment penalties are allowed in some form (but not necessarily imposed) in thirty-six states and the District of Columbia.

Principal: the amount of debt, not counting interest, left on a loan.

Private mortgage insurance (PMI): in the event that you do not have a twenty percent down payment, lenders will allow a smaller one—as low as 5 percent in some cases. With the smaller down-payment loans, however, borrowers are usually required to carry private mortgage insurance. This requires an initial premium payment of one to five percent of your mortgage amount and may require an additional monthly fee depending on your loan's structure. On a $75,000 house with a 10 percent down payment, this would mean either an initial premium payment of $2,025 to $3,375, or an initial premium of $675 to $1,130 combined with a monthly payment of $25 to $30.

Realtor: a real estate broker or an associate holding active membership in a local real estate board affiliated with the National Association of Realtors.

Recision: the cancellation of a contract. With respect to mortgage refinancing, the law that gives a homeowner three days to cancel a contract in some cases once it is signed if the transaction uses equity in the home as security.

Recording fees: money paid to the lender for recording a home sale with the local authorities, thereby making it part of the public records.

Renegotiable-rate mortgage (RRM): a loan in which the interest rate is adjusted periodically. See *adjustable-rate mortgage.*

RESPA: short for Real Estate Settlement Procedures Act. RESPA is a federal law that allows consumers to review information on known estimated settlement costs once after application and once prior to or at settlement. The law requires lenders to furnish the information after application only.

Reverse-annuity mortgage (RAM): a form of mortgage in which the lender makes periodic payments to the borrower using the borrower's equity in the home as security.

Servicing: all the steps and operations a lender performs to keep a loan in good standing, such as collection of payments, payment of taxes, insurance, property inspections, and the like.

Settlement/Settlement costs: see *closing/closing costs.*

Shared-appreciation mortgage (SAM): a mortgage in which a borrower receives a below-market interest rate in return for which the lender (or another investor such as a family member or other partner) receives a portion of the future appreciation in the value of the property. May also apply to mortgages in which a borrower shares the monthly principal and interest payments with another party in exchange for a part of the appreciation.

Survey: a measurement of land, prepared by a registered land surveyor, showing the location of the land with reference to known points, its dimensions, and the location and dimensions of any buildings.

Term mortgage: see *balloon (payment) mortgage.*

Title: a document that gives evidence of an individual's ownership of property.

Title insurance: a policy, usually issued by a title-insurance company, that insures a home buyer against errors in the title search. The cost of the policy is usually a function of the value of the property, and is often borne by the purchaser and/or seller.

Title search: an examination of municipal records to determine the legal ownership of property. Usually is performed by a title company.

Truth-in-lending: a federal law requiring disclosure of the annual percentage rate to home buyers shortly after they apply for the loan.

Two-step mortgage: a mortgage in which the borrower receives a below-market interest rate for a specified number of years (most often seven or ten) and then receives a new interest rate adjusted (within certain limits) to market conditions at that time. The lender sometimes has the option to call the loan due with thirty days' notice at the end of seven or ten years. Also called "super seven" or "premier" mortgage.

Underwriting: the decision whether to make a loan to a potential home buyer based on credit, employment, assets, and other factors, and the matching of this risk to an appropriate rate and term or loan amount.

VA loan: a long-term, low- or no-down-payment loan guaranteed by the Department of Veterans Affairs. Restricted to individuals qualified by military service or other entitlements.

VA mortgage funding fee: a premium of up to $1\frac{7}{8}$ percent (depending on the size of the down payment) paid on a VA-backed loan. On a $75,000 thirty-year fixed-rate mortgage with no down payment, this would amount to $1,406 either paid at closing or added to the amount financed.

Variable-rate mortgage (VRM): see *adjustable rate mortgage.*

Verification of deposit (VOD): a document signed by the borrower's financial institution verifying the status and balance of his/her financial accounts.

Verification of employment (VOE): a document signed by the borrower's employer verifying his or her position and salary.

Wraparound: when an existing assumable loan is combined with a new loan, it results in an interest rate somewhere between the old rate and the current market rate. The payments are made to a second lender or the previous homeowner, who then forwards the payments to the first lender after taking the additional amount off the top.

Index